Confessions of
a Book Lover

RUSKIN BOND

Confessions of a Book Lover

PENGUIN
VIKING
An imprint of Penguin Random House

VIKING

USA | Canada | UK | Ireland | Australia
New Zealand | India | South Africa | China | Singapore

Viking is part of the Penguin Random House group of companies
whose addresses can be found at global.penguinrandomhouse.com

Published by Penguin Random House India Pvt. Ltd
4th Floor, Capital Tower 1, MG Road,
Gurugram 122 002, Haryana, India

First published in Viking by Penguin Random House India 2017

Copyright © Ruskin Bond 2017

All rights reserved

10 9 8 7 6 5 4 3 2

ISBN 9780670088980

Typeset in Adobe Garamond Pro by Manipal Digital Systems, Manipal
Printed at Replika Press Pvt. Ltd, India

This book is sold subject to the condition that it shall not, by way of trade or otherwise,
be lent, resold, hired out, or otherwise circulated without the publisher's prior consent
in any form of binding or cover other than that in which it is published and without a
similar condition including this condition being imposed on the subsequent purchaser.

www.penguin.co.in

This is a legitimate digitally printed version of the book and therefore might not
have certain extra finishing on the cover.

Contents

Contents

Introduction

About two years ago Penguin India indulged one of my whims by allowing me to put together a collection of extracts from some of the books that had given me pleasure and delight over the years. It was called *Love Among the Bookshelves*, and each extract was fronted by an essay in which I described how I first encountered the book and what it meant to me at the time.

We did not expect the anthology to soar into the bestseller lists, and were pleasantly surprised when the book went into several impressions. Obviously there were readers out there who were interested in discovering or renewing their acquaintance with some of the past masters—writers whose individual style and literary qualities had set them apart: Charles Dickens, P.G. Wodehouse, Somerset Maugham, H.E. Bates, Richard Jeffries.

Encouraged by its reception, I have had the temerity to bring out a sequel—a further selection of old favourites (mine, of course!) in the hope that readers will either go back to these fine writers or start hunting for their works on the Internet or on old library shelves. Here then are gems from Joseph Conrad, H.G. Wells, George and Weedon Grossmith, William Saroyan, Jack London and others. So who's afraid of Virginia Woolf? You won't be, once you have read this memorable piece of historical writing. And you will want to read more by that wicked person, Laurence Sterne, whose 'Sentimental Journey' frequently takes him into the wrong bedroom.

Once again, I have fronted each story or extract with a little essay of my own, for these writers were important to me at various stages of my personal and writing life. My only regret is that I have had to leave out other favourites— R.L. Stevenson, Walter de la Mare, Rabindranath Tagore, Andre Gide, George Orwell . . . the list goes on and on.

So beware, dear reader. A third compilation might well be around the corner!

Landour, Mussoorie   Ruskin Bond
25 March 2017

1

Radio Times

In that winter of 1948–49 I was just fourteen years old, but I was doing a tremendous amount of reading, as I had no friends and my feelings towards my mother and stepfather were not exactly affectionate. I read whatever literature came my way, and this included *The Complete Works of Shakespeare* and bound copies of the *Daily Mirror* (several months old), which were available from the newsagents.

I read all the plays, rather wearily at times, but I had given myself this as a task of sorts, and so I suffered bravely through *Coriolanus* and *Titus Andronicus* and some of those tedious English kings. The language was superb but the plots certainly creaked. I've always wondered why every *Complete Shakespeare* has to include that unpleasant poem, *The Rape of Lucrece*, at the end; I can't believe it was written by the same person.

My favourite play was *The Tempest*. It had a certain magic, but I was happy to complete my self-appointed task and get back to reading the works of mere mortals.

And what would I have done without my short-wave radio? Every evening I would tune in to the Overseas

Service of the BBC to listen to the comedy programmes that were a regular feature on the air waves. There was Tommy Handley in *ITMA* (*It's That Man Again*); Eric Barker in *Waterlogged Spa*; and Richard Murdoch and Kenneth Horne in *Much-Binding-in-the-Marsh*. *Much-Binding* was a glorious romp in an English village; no satire there. But *ITMA* had Colonel Chinstrap, a pompous ass, and Funf, a villainous character of indeterminate nationality. That was the age of the radio, and these comedy shows were classics of their kind. I never tired of listening to them. If I was depressed, they cheered me up and made me laugh. They even taught me to laugh at myself, to look on the bright side of life and living; and to realize that the world was a ridiculous sort of place, full of demented leaders like Hitler and fat dictators like Mussolini, all destined to come to a sticky end sooner or later but not before they had done their best to turn the world upside down. A world full of egotists, but the best comedians knew how to prick the bubble of their egotism.

In a *Daily Mirror* I came across an interview with Tommy Handley in which, when asked to name his favourite humorous book, he spoke of *The Diary of a Nobody*. I had never heard of it, but I learnt that it had been written in the 1890s by George and Weedon Grossmith, both of whom had been active in the theatre. In fact,

George Grossmith was almost always the lead actor and singer in the Gilbert and Sullivan operettas of that period. They were also contributors to *Punch*—Weedon being the illustrator—and *The Diary* had first appeared in that popular compendium of English humour.

I resolved to obtain a copy of *The Diary of a Nobody*, but it wasn't available in Dehradun; nor could it be found in my school library. But on a visit to a Simla bookshop I found the Everyman edition, a new copy, and I spent all my pocket money in order to buy it.

Nor was I disappointed. Mr. Pooter, a figure of fun to everyone but himself, has been a friend to me over the years, and I turn to his exploits (or lack of them) whenever I am in the dumps. Not everyone finds *The Diary of a Nobody* funny. It is not the humour of *Three Men in a Boat*; nor is it the humour of P.G. Wodehouse's *Blandings Castle*. It is, in fact, rather hard to define its humour. It's the portrait (or self-portrait) of a Victorian city clerk who takes himself rather too seriously; and makes an ass of himself in the process. And here he is, in this extract, having some difficulty in recovering from a hangover.

From *The Diary of a Nobody* (1892)
by George and Weedon Grossmith

I

AFTER THE MANSION HOUSE BALL. CARRIE
OFFENDED. GOWING ALSO OFFENDED.
A PLEASANT PARTY AT THE CUMMINGS'.
MR. FRANCHING, OF PECKHAM, VISITS US

MAY 8.—I woke up with a most terrible headache. I could
scarcely see, and the back of my neck was as if I had given
it a crick. I thought first of sending for a doctor; but I did
not think it necessary. When up, I felt faint, and went to
Brownish's, the chemist, who gave me a draught. So bad at
the office, had to get leave to come home. Went to another
chemist in the City, and I got a draught. Brownish's dose
seems to have made me worse; have eaten nothing all day.
To make matters worse, Carrie, every time I spoke to her,
answered me sharply—that is, when she answered at all.

In the evening I felt very much worse again and said
to her: "I do believe I've been poisoned by the lobster
mayonnaise at the Mansion House last night"; she

simply replied, without taking her eyes from her sewing: "Champagne never did agree with you." I felt irritated, and said: "What nonsense you talk; I only had a glass and a half, and you know as well as I do—" Before I could complete the sentence she bounced out of the room. I sat over an hour waiting for her to return; but as she did not, I determined I would go to bed. I discovered Carrie had gone to bed without even saying "good night"; leaving me to bar the scullery door and feed the cat. I shall certainly speak to her about this in the morning.

MAY 9.—Still a little shaky, with black specks. The *Blackfriars Bi-weekly News* contains a long list of the guests at the Mansion House Ball. Disappointed to find our names omitted, though Farmerson's is in plainly enough with M.L.L. after it, whatever that may mean. More than vexed, because we had ordered a dozen copies to send to our friends. Wrote to the *Blackfriars Bi-weekly News*, pointing out their omission.

Carrie had commenced her breakfast when I entered the parlour. I helped myself to a cup of tea, and I said, perfectly calmly and quietly: "Carrie, I wish a little explanation of your conduct last night."

She replied, "Indeed! and I desire something more than a *little* explanation of your conduct the night before."

I said, coolly: "Really, I don't understand you."

Carrie said sneeringly: "Probably not; you were scarcely in a condition to understand anything."

I was astounded at this insinuation and simply ejaculated: "Caroline!"

She said: "Don't be theatrical, it has no effect on me. Reserve that tone for your new friend, *Mister* Farmerson, the ironmonger."

I was about to speak, when Carrie, in a temper such as I have never seen her in before, told me to hold my tongue. She said: "Now *I'm* going to say something! After professing to snub Mr. Farmerson, you permit him to snub *you*, in my presence, and then accept his invitation to take a glass of champagne with you, and you don't limit yourself to one glass. You then offer this vulgar man, who made a bungle of repairing our scraper, a seat in our cab on the way home. I say nothing about his tearing my dress in getting in the cab, nor of treading on Mrs. James's expensive fan, which you knocked out of my hand, and for which he never even apologised; but you smoked all the way home without having the decency to ask my permission. That is not all! At the end of the journey, although he did not offer you a farthing towards his share of the cab, you asked him in. Fortunately, he was sober enough to detect, from my manner, that his company was not desirable."

Goodness knows I felt humiliated enough at this; but, to make matters worse, Gowing entered the room, without knocking, with two hats on his head and holding the garden rake in his hand, with Carrie's fur tippet (which he had taken off the downstairs hall-peg) round his neck, and announced himself in a loud, coarse voice: "His Royal Highness, the Lord Mayor!" He marched twice round the room like a buffoon, and finding we took no notice, said: "Hulloh! what's up? Lovers' quarrel, eh?"

There was silence for a moment, so I said quietly: "My dear Gowing, I'm not very well, and not quite in the humour for joking; especially when you enter the room without knocking, an act which I fail to see the fun of."

Gowing said: "I'm very sorry, but I called for my stick, which I thought you would have sent round." I handed him his stick, which I remembered I had painted black with the enamel paint, thinking to improve it. He looked at it for a minute with a dazed expression and said: "Who did this?"

I said: "Eh, did what?"

He said: "Did what? Why, destroyed my stick! It belonged to my poor uncle, and I value it more than anything I have in the world! I'll know who did it."

I said: "I'm very sorry. I dare say it will come off. I did it for the best."

Gowing said: "Then all I can say is, it's a confounded liberty; and I *would* add, you're a bigger fool than you look, only *that's* absolutely impossible."

MAY 12.—Got a single copy of the *Blackfriars Bi-weekly News*. There was a short list of several names they had omitted; but the stupid people had mentioned our names as "Mr. and Mrs. C. Porter." Most annoying! Wrote again and I took particular care to write our name in capital letters, *POOTER*, so that there should be no possible mistake this time.

MAY 16.—Absolutely disgusted on opening the *Blackfriars Bi-weekly News* of to-day, to find the following paragraph: "We have received two letters from Mr. and Mrs. Charles Pewter, requesting us to announce the important fact that they were at the Mansion House Ball." I tore up the paper and threw it in the waste-paper basket. My time is far too valuable to bother about such trifles.

MAY 21.—The last week or ten days terribly dull, Carrie being away at Mrs. James's, at Sutton. Cummings also away. Gowing, I presume, is still offended with me for black-enamelling his stick without asking him.

MAY 22.—Purchased a new stick mounted with silver, which cost seven-and-sixpence (shall tell Carrie five shillings), and sent it round with nice note to Gowing.

MAY 23.—Received strange note from Gowing; he said: "Offended? not a bit, my boy. I thought you were offended with me for losing my temper. Besides, I found, after all, it was not my poor old uncle's stick you painted. It was only a shilling thing I bought at a tobacconist's. However, I am much obliged to you for your handsome present all same."

MAY 24.—Carrie back. Hoorah! She looks wonderfully well, except that the sun has caught her nose.

MAY 25.—Carrie brought down some of my shirts and advised me to take them to Trillip's round the corner. She said: "The fronts and cuffs are much frayed." I said without a moment's hesitation: "I'm *frayed* they are." Lor! how we roared. I thought we should never stop laughing. As I happened to be sitting next the driver going to town on the 'bus, I told him my joke about the "frayed" shirts. I thought he would have rolled off his seat. They laughed at the office a good bit too over it.

MAY 26.—Left the shirts to be repaired at Trillip's. I said to him: "I'm 'fraid they are *frayed*." He said, without a smile:

"They're bound to do that, sir." Some people seem to be quite destitute of a sense of humour.

JUNE 1.—The last week has been like old times, Carrie being back, and Gowing and Cummings calling every evening nearly. Twice we sat out in the garden quite late. This evening we were like a pack of children, and played "consequences." It is a good game.

JUNE 2.—"Consequences" again this evening. Not quite so successful as last night; Gowing having several times overstepped the limits of good taste.

JUNE 4.—In the evening Carrie and I went round to Mr. and Mrs. Cummings' to spend a quiet evening with them. Gowing was there, also Mr. Stillbrook. It was quiet but pleasant. Mrs. Cummings sang five or six songs, "No, Sir," and "The Garden of Sleep," being best in my humble judgment; but what pleased me most was the duet she sang with Carrie—classical duet, too. I think it is called, "I would that my love!" It was beautiful. If Carrie had been in better voice, I don't think professionals could have sung it better. After supper we made them sing it again. I never liked Mr. Stillbrook since the walk that Sunday to the "Cow and Hedge," but I must say he sings comic-songs well. His song: "We don't Want the old men now," made us shriek with laughter, especially the verse referring to Mr. Gladstone; but there was one verse I think he might have omitted, and I said so, but Gowing thought it was the best of the lot.

JUNE 6.—Trillip brought round the shirts and, to my disgust, his charge for repairing was more than I gave for them when new. I told him so, and he impertinently replied: "Well, they are better now than when they were new." I paid him, and said it was a robbery. He said: "If you wanted your shirt-fronts made out of pauper-linen, such as is used for packing and book-binding, why didn't you say so?"

JUNE 7.—A dreadful annoyance. Met Mr. Franching, who lives at Peckham, and who is a great swell in his way. I ventured to ask him to come home to meat-tea, and take pot-luck. I did not think he would accept such a humble invitation; but he did, saying, in a most friendly way, he would rather "peck" with us than by himself. I said: "We had better get into this blue 'bus." He replied: "No blue-bussing for me. I have had enough of the blues lately. I lost a cool 'thou' over the Copper Scare. Step in here."

We drove up home in style, in a hansom-cab, and I knocked three times at the front door without getting an answer. I saw Carrie, through the panels of ground-glass (with stars), rushing upstairs. I told Mr. Franching to wait at the door while I went round to the side. There I saw the grocer's boy actually picking off the paint on the door, which had formed into blisters. No time to reprove him; so went round and effected an entrance through the kitchen window. I let in Mr. Franching, and showed him into the drawing-room. I went upstairs to Carrie, who was changing her dress, and told her I had persuaded Mr. Franching to come home. She replied: "How can you do such a thing? You know it's Sarah's holiday, and there's not a thing in the house, the cold mutton having turned with the hot weather."

Eventually Carrie, like a good creature as she is, slipped down, washed up the teacups, and laid the cloth, and I gave Franching our views of Japan to look at while I ran round to the butcher's to get three chops.

July 30.—The miserable cold weather is either upsetting me or Carrie, or both. We seem to break out into an argument about absolutely nothing, and this unpleasant state of things usually occurs at meal-times.

This morning, for some unaccountable reason, we were talking about balloons, and we were as merry as possible;

but the conversation drifted into family matters, during which Carrie, without the slightest reason, referred in the most uncomplimentary manner to my poor father's pecuniary trouble. I retorted by saying that "Pa, at all events, was a gentleman," whereupon Carrie burst out crying. I positively could not eat any breakfast.

At the office I was sent for by Mr. Perkupp, who said he was very sorry, but I should have to take my annual holidays from next Saturday. Franching called at office and asked me to dine at his club, "The Constitutional." Fearing disagreeables at home after the "tiff" this morning, I sent a telegram to Carrie, telling her I was going out to dine and she was not to sit up. Bought a little silver bangle for Carrie.

JULY 31.—Carrie was very pleased with the bangle, which I left with an affectionate note on her dressing-table last night before going to bed. I told Carrie we should have to start for our holiday next Saturday. She replied quite happily that she did not mind, except that the weather was so bad, and she feared that Miss Jibbons would not be able to get her a seaside dress in time. I told Carrie that I thought the drab one with pink bows looked quite good enough; and Carrie said she should not think of wearing it. I was about to discuss the matter, when, remembering the argument yesterday, resolved to hold my tongue.

I said to Carrie: "I don't think we can do better than 'Good old Broadstairs.'" Carrie not only, to my astonishment, raised an objection to Broadstairs, for the first time; but begged me not to use the expression, "Good old," but to leave it to Mr. Stillbrook and other *gentlemen* of his type. Hearing my 'bus pass the window, I was obliged to rush out of the house without kissing Carrie as usual; and I shouted to her: "I leave it to you to decide." On returning in the evening, Carrie said she thought as the time was so short she had decided on Broadstairs, and had written to Mrs. Beck, Harbour View Terrace, for apartments.

AUGUST 1.—Ordered a new pair of trousers at Edwards's, and told them not to cut them so loose over the boot; the last pair being so loose and also tight at the knee, looked like a sailor's, and I heard Pitt, that objectionable youth at the office, call out "Hornpipe" as I passed his desk. Carrie has ordered of Miss Jibbons a pink Garibaldi and blue-serge skirt, which I always think looks so pretty at the seaside. In the evening she trimmed herself a little sailor-hat, while I read to her the *Exchange and Mart*. We had a good laugh over my trying on the hat when she had finished it; Carrie saying it looked so funny with my beard, and how the people would have roared if I went on the stage like it.

AUGUST 2.—Mrs. Beck wrote to say we could have our usual rooms at Broadstairs. That's off our mind. Bought a coloured shirt and a pair of tan-coloured boots, which I see many of the swell clerks wearing in the City, and hear are all the "go."

AUGUST 3.—A beautiful day. Looking forward to tomorrow. Carrie bought a parasol about five feet long. I told her it was ridiculous. She said: "Mrs. James, of Sutton, has one twice as long"; so the matter dropped. I bought a capital hat for hot weather at the seaside. I don't know what it is called, but it is the shape of the helmet worn in India, only made of straw. Got three new ties, two coloured handkerchiefs, and a pair of navy-blue socks at Pope Brothers. Spent the evening packing. Carrie told me not to forget to borrow Mr. Higgsworth's telescope, which he always lends me, knowing I know how to take care of it. Sent Sarah out for it. While everything was seeming so bright, the last post brought us a letter from Mrs. Beck, saying: "I have just let all my house to one party, and am sorry I must take back my words, and am sorry you must find other apartments; but Mrs. Womming, next door, will be pleased to accommodate you, but she cannot take you before Monday, as her rooms are engaged Bank Holiday week."

II

THE UNEXPECTED ARRIVAL HOME OF OUR SON, WILLIE LUPIN POOTER

AUGUST 4.—The first post brought a nice letter from our dear son Willie, acknowledging a trifling present which Carrie sent him, the day before yesterday being his twentieth birthday. To our utter amazement he turned up himself in the afternoon, having journeyed all the way from Oldham. He said he had got leave from the bank, and as Monday was a holiday he thought he would give us a little surprise.

AUGUST 5, SUNDAY.—We have not seen Willie since last Christmas, and are pleased to notice what a fine young man he has grown. One would scarcely believe he was Carrie's son. He looks more like a younger brother. I rather disapprove of his wearing a check suit on a Sunday, and I think he ought to have gone to church this morning; but he said he was tired after yesterday's journey, so I refrained from any remark on the subject. We had a bottle of port for dinner, and drank dear Willie's health.

He said: "Oh, by-the-by, did I tell you I've cut my first name, 'William,' and taken the second name 'Lupin'? In fact, I'm only known at Oldham as 'Lupin Pooter.' If you were to 'Willie' me there, they wouldn't know what you meant."

Of course, Lupin being a purely family name, Carrie was delighted, and began by giving a long history of the Lupins. I ventured to say that I thought William a nice simple name, and reminded him he was christened after his Uncle William, who was much respected in the City. Willie, in a manner which I did not much care for, said sneeringly: "Oh, I know all about that—Good old Bill!" and helped himself to a third glass of port.

Carrie objected strongly to my saying "Good old," but she made no remark when Willie used the double adjective. I said nothing, but looked at her, which meant more. I said: "My dear Willie, I hope you are happy with your colleagues at the Bank." He replied: "Lupin, if you please; and with respect to the Bank, there's not a clerk who is a gentleman, and the 'boss' is a cad." I felt so shocked, I could say nothing, and my instinct told me there was something wrong.

AUGUST 6, BANK HOLIDAY.—As there was no sign of Lupin moving at nine o'clock, I knocked at his door, and said we usually breakfasted at half-past eight, and asked how long would he be? Lupin replied that he had had a lively time of it, first with the train shaking the house all night, and then with the sun streaming in through the window in his eyes, and giving him a cracking headache. Carrie came up and asked if he would like some breakfast sent up, and he said he could do with a cup of tea, and didn't want anything to eat.

Lupin not having come down, I went up again at half-past one, and said we dined at two; he said he "would be there." He never came down till a quarter to three. I said: "We have not seen much of you, and you will have to return by the 5.30 train; therefore you will have to leave in an hour, unless you go by the midnight mail." He said: "Look here, Guv'nor, it's no use beating about the bush. I've tendered my resignation at the Bank."

For a moment I could not speak. When my speech came again, I said: "How dare you, sir? How dare you take such a serious step without consulting me? Don't answer me, sir!—you will sit down immediately, and write a note at my dictation, withdrawing your resignation and amply apologising for your thoughtlessness."

Imagine my dismay when he replied with a loud guffaw: "It's no use. If you want the good old truth, I've got the chuck!"

AUGUST 7.—Mr. Perkupp has given me leave to postpone my holiday a week, as we could not get the room. This will give us an opportunity of trying to find an appointment for Willie before we go. The ambition of my life would be to get him into Mr. Perkupp's firm.

AUGUST 11.—Although it is a serious matter having our boy Lupin on our hands, still it is satisfactory to know he was asked to resign from the Bank simply because "he took no interest in his work, and always arrived an hour (sometimes two hours) late." We can all start off on Monday to Broadstairs with a light heart. This will take my mind off the worry of the last few days, which have been wasted over a useless correspondence with the manager of the Bank at Oldham.

AUGUST 13.—Hurrah! at Broadstairs. Very nice apartments near the station. On the cliffs they would have been double the price. The landlady had a nice five-o'clock dinner and tea ready, which we all enjoyed, though Lupin seemed fastidious because there happened to be a fly in the butter. It was very wet in the evening, for which I was thankful, as it was a good excuse for going to bed early. Lupin said he would sit up and read a bit.

AUGUST 14.—I was a little annoyed to find Lupin, instead of reading last night, had gone to a common sort of entertainment, given at the Assembly Rooms. I expressed my opinion that such performances were unworthy of respectable patronage; but he replied: "Oh, it was only 'for one night only.' I had a fit of the blues come on, and thought I would go to see Polly Presswell, England's Particular Spark." I told him I was proud to say I had never heard of her. Carrie said: "Do let the boy alone. He's quite old enough to take care of himself, and won't forget he's a gentleman. Remember, you were young once yourself." Rained all day hard, but Lupin would go out.

AUGUST 15.—Cleared up a bit, so we all took the train to Margate, and the first person we met on the jetty was Gowing. I said: "Hulloh! I thought you had gone to Barmouth with your Birmingham friends?" He said: "Yes, but young Peter Lawrence was so ill, they postponed their visit, so I came down here. You know the Cummings' are here too?" Carrie said: "Oh, that will be delightful! We must have some evenings together and have games."

I introduced Lupin, saying: "You will be pleased to find we have our dear boy at home!" Gowing said: "How's that? You don't mean to say he's left the Bank?"

I changed the subject quickly, and thereby avoided any of those awkward questions which Gowing always has a knack of asking.

AUGUST 16.—Lupin positively refused to walk down the Parade with me because I was wearing my new straw helmet with my frock-coat. I don't know what the boy is coming to.

AUGUST 17.—Lupin not falling in with our views, Carrie and I went for a sail. It was a relief to be with her alone; for when Lupin irritates me, she always sides with him. On our return, he said: "Oh, you've been on the 'Shilling Emetic,' have you? You'll come to six-pennorth on the 'Liver Jerker' next." I presume he meant a tricycle, but I affected not to understand him.

AUGUST 18.—Gowing and Cummings walked over to arrange an evening at Margate. It being wet, Gowing asked Cummings to accompany him to the hotel and have a game of billiards, knowing I never play, and in fact disapprove of the game. Cummings said he must hasten back to Margate; whereupon Lupin, to my horror, said: "I'll give you a game, Gowing—a hundred up. A walk round the cloth will give me an appetite for dinner." I said: "Perhaps *Mister* Gowing does not care to play with boys." Gowing surprised me by saying: "Oh yes, I do, if they play well," and they walked off together.

AUGUST 19, SUNDAY.—I was about to read Lupin a sermon on smoking (which he indulges in violently) and billiards, but he put on his hat and walked out. Carrie then read *me* a long sermon on the palpable inadvisability of treating Lupin as if he were a mere child. I felt she was somewhat right, so in the evening I offered him a cigar. He seemed pleased, but, after a few whiffs, said: "This is a good old tup'ny—try one of mine," and he handed me a cigar as long as it was strong, which is saying a good deal.

AUGUST 20.—I am glad our last day at the seaside was fine, though clouded overhead. We went over to Cummings' (at Margate) in the evening, and as it was cold, we stayed in and played games; Gowing, as usual, overstepping the mark. He suggested we should play "Cutlets," a game we never heard of. He sat on a chair, and asked Carrie to sit on his lap, an invitation which dear Carrie rightly declined.

After some species of wrangling, *I* sat on Gowing's knees and Carrie sat on the edge of mine. Lupin sat on the edge of Carrie's lap, then Cummings on Lupin's, and Mrs. Cummings on her husband's. We looked very ridiculous, and laughed a good deal.

Gowing then said: "Are you a believer in the Great Mogul?" We had to answer all together: "Yes—oh, yes!" (three times). Gowing said: "So am I," and suddenly got up. The result of this stupid joke was that we all fell on the ground, and poor Carrie banged her head against the corner of the fender. Mrs. Cummings put some vinegar on; but through this we missed the last train, and had to drive back to Broadstairs, which cost me seven-and-sixpence.

2

Humour in a Hospital Bed

In the summer of 1949, while we were in rehearsals for the school play, I contracted jaundice. My pee became a dark amber in colour, I developed a low fever, and felt weak and lethargic most of the time. But I did not report sick, just hung on till the play was performed. It was a farce called *Tons of Money*, and I had a fairly important part, playing another character's double. For this I had to wear a false beard. Being unwell, I did not stick it on properly, and it kept coming unstuck during the play, which only added to the comedy. The proceedings were far from funny for me, however, and when the curtain finally came down I missed the curtain-call because I was busy vomiting offstage. I spent the night in the school infirmary and was then shifted to Simla's Ripon Hospital, a crowded government institution. My condition was quite serious and for two nights I could not sleep due to abdominal pains. I was transferred from the general ward to a small private room, and treated with Dr Beerhan's Liver Pills to increase the flow of bile. Maybe this did the trick because I made a slow but steady recovery.

There were not many English-reading patients in the Ripon Hospital in 1949, but a kind matron discovered a cache of old books in the staffroom cupboard and had them sent to me on a trolley. Most of the books were of a humorous nature, obviously selected to raise the spirits of depressed doctors, nurses and patients. It was among these that I discovered the works of Barry Pain, Arthur Morrison (*Tales of Mean Streets*), Saki, O. Henry and Stacy Aumonier. There were also piles of back issues of *Punch*, and although I did not care much for the articles (which, being topical, had dated over the years), I enjoyed the cartoons and read all the book and film reviews.

Among the humorous writers, I found Stacy Aumonier's stories the most entertaining. In the early years of the nineteenth century he had made a living as a 'society entertainer', a raconteur and pioneering stand-up comedian; and when this form of entertainment went out of fashion, he turned to short story writing with considerable success. Unfortunately his output was not very large, as he died at the age of forty. I have read some of his stories twice over and they are always a joy to read. *Miss Bracegirdle Does Her Duty* is one of my favourites. A strait-laced English maiden lady on her first trip to France finds herself caught up in a sensational scandal.

Read on . . .

'Miss Bracegirdle Does Her Duty' (1916)
by Stacy Aumonier

STACY AUMONIER (1887–1928) *had a varied career before he finally settled down to make his name as a novelist and writer of short stories. The son of an architectural sculptor, he became a decorative designer and landscape painter, but his wit as a raconteur and his charm of manner led him to become a society entertainer at a time when that profession was fast dying out, before be 'found himself' as a storyteller!*

"This is the room, madame."

"Ah, thank you—thank you."

"Does it appear satisfactory to madame?"

"Oh, yes. Thank you—quite."

"Does madame require anything further?"

"Er—if not too late, may I have a hot bath?"

"*Parfaitement*, madame. The bathroom is at the end of the passage on the left. I will go and prepare it for madame."

"There is one thing more. I have had a very long journey. I am very tired. Will you please see that I am not disturbed in the morning until I ring?"

"Certainly, madame."

Millicent Bracegirdle *was* speaking the truth—she *was* tired. But then, in the sleepy cathedral town of Easingstoke, from which she came, it was customary for everyone to speak the truth. It was customary, moreover, for everyone to lead simple, self-denying lives—to give up their time to good works and elevating thoughts. One had only to glance at little Miss Bracegirdle to see that in her were epitomised all the virtues and ideals of Easingstoke.

Indeed, it was the pursuit of duty which had brought her to the Hôtel de l'Ouest at Bordeaux on this summer's night. She had travelled from Easingstoke to London, then without a break to Dover, crossed that horrid stretch of sea to Calais, entrained for Paris, where of necessity she had to spend four hours—a terrifying experience—and then had come on to Bordeaux, arriving at midnight. The reason of this journey being that someone had to come to Bordeaux to meet her young sister-in-law, who was arriving the next day from South America. The sister-in-law was married to a missionary in Paraguay, but the climate not agreeing with her, she was returning to England. Her dear brother, the dean, would have come himself, but the claims on his time were so extensive, the parishioners would miss him so—it was clearly Millicent's duty to go.

She had never been out of England before, and she had a horror of travel, and an ingrained distrust of foreigners. She spoke a little French, sufficient for the purpose of travel and for obtaining any modest necessities, but not sufficient for carrying on any kind of conversation. She did not deplore this latter fact, for she was of opinion that French people were not the kind of people that one would naturally want to have conversation with; broadly speaking, they were not quite "nice," in spite of their ingratiating manners.

She unpacked her valise, placed her things about the room, tried to thrust back the little stabs of home-sickness as she visualised her darling room at the deanery. How strange and hard and unfriendly seemed these foreign hotel bedrooms! No chintz and lavender and photographs of all the dear family, the dean, the nephews and nieces, the interior of the Cathedral during harvest festival; no samplers and needlework or coloured reproductions of the paintings by Marcus Stone. Oh, dear, how foolish she was! What *did* she expect?

She disrobed, and donned a dressing-gown; then, armed with a sponge-bag and towel, she crept timidly down the passage to the bathroom, after closing her bedroom door and turning out the light. The gay bathroom cheered her. She wallowed luxuriously in the hot water, regarding her slim legs with quiet satisfaction. And for the first time since leaving home there came to her a pleasant moment, a sense of enjoyment in her adventure. After all, it *was* rather an adventure, and her life had been peculiarly devoid of it. What queer lives some people must live, travelling about, having experiences! How old was she? Not really old—not by any means. Forty-two? Forty-three? She had shut herself up so. She hardly ever regarded the potentialities of age. As the world went, she was a well-preserved woman for her age. A life of self-abnegation, simple living, healthy walking, and fresh air had kept her younger than these hurrying, pampered, city people.

Love? Yes, once when she was a young girl—he was a schoolmaster, a most estimable, kind gentleman. They were never engaged—not actually, but it was a kind of understood thing. For three years it went on, this pleasant understanding and friendship. He was so gentle, so distinguished and considerate. She would have been happy to have continued in this strain for ever. But there was something lacking—Stephen had curious restless lapses. From the physical aspect of marriage she shrank—yes, even with Stephen, who was gentleness and kindness itself. And then, one day—one day he went away, vanished, and never returned. They told her he had married one of the country girls, a girl who used to work in Mrs. Forbes's dairy—not a very nice girl, she feared, one of those fast, pretty, foolish women. Heigho! Well, she had lived that down, destructive as the blow appeared at the time. One lives everything down in time. There is always work, living for others, faith, duty. At the same time she could sympathise with people who found satisfaction in unusual experiences. There would be lots to tell the dear dean when she wrote to him on the morrow: nearly losing her spectacles on the restaurant-car, the amusing remarks of an American child on the train to Paris, the curious food everywhere, nothing simple and plain; the two English ladies at the hotel in Paris who told her about the death of their uncle—the poor man being taken ill on Friday and dying on Sunday afternoon, just before tea-time; the kindness of the hotel proprietor, who had sat up for her; the prettiness of the chambermaid. Oh, yes, everyone was really very kind. The French people, after all, were very nice. She had seen nothing—nothing but what was quite nice and decorous. There would be lots to tell the dean to-morrow.

Her body glowed with the friction of the towel. She again donned her night attire and her thick woollen dressing-gown. She tidied up the bathroom carefully in exactly the same way she was accustomed to do at home; then once more gripped her sponge-bag and towel, and turning out the light she crept down the passage to her room. Entering the room, she switched on the light and shut the door quickly. Then one of those ridiculous things happened, just the kind of thing you would expect to happen in a foreign hotel. The handle of the door came off in her hand. She ejaculated a quiet "Bother!" and sought to replace it with one hand, the other being occupied with the towel and sponge-bag. In doing this she behaved foolishly, for, thrusting the knob carelessly against the steel pin without properly securing it, she only succeeded in pushing the pin farther into the door, and the knob was not adjusted. She uttered another little "Bother!" and put her sponge-bag and towel down on the floor. She then tried to recover the pin with her left hand, but it had gone in too far.

"How very foolish!" she thought. "I shall have to ring for the chambermaid—and perhaps the poor girl has gone to bed."

She turned and faced the room, and suddenly the awful horror was upon her.

There was a man asleep in her bed!

The sight of that swarthy face on the pillow, with its black tousled hair and heavy moustache, produced in her the most terrible moment of her life. Her heart nearly stopped. For some seconds she could neither think nor scream, and her first thought was:

"I mustn't scream!"

She stood there like one paralysed, staring at the man's head and the great curved hunch of his body under the clothes. When she began to think she thought very quickly and all her thoughts worked together. The first vivid realisation was that it wasn't the man's fault; it was *her* fault. *She was in the wrong room.* It was the man's room. The rooms were identical, but there were all his things about, his clothes thrown carelessly over chairs, his collar and tie on the wardrobe, his great heavy boots and the strange yellow trunk. She must get out—somehow, anyhow. She clutched once more at the door, feverishly driving her fingernails into the hole where the elusive pin had vanished. She tried to force her fingers in the crack and open the door that way, but it was of no avail. She was to all intents and purposes locked in—locked in a bedroom in a strange hotel, alone with a man—a foreigner—a *Frenchman*!

She must think—she must think! She switched off the light. If the light was off he might not wake up. It might give her time to think how to act. It was surprising that he had not awakened. If he *did* wake up, what would he do? How could she explain herself? He wouldn't believe her. No one would believe her. In an English hotel it would be difficult enough, but here, where she wasn't known, where they were all foreigners and consequently antagonistic— merciful heavens!

She *must* get out. Should she wake the man? No, she couldn't do that. He might murder her. He might—oh, it was too awful to contemplate! Should she scream? Ring for the chambermaid? But no; it would be the same thing. People would come rushing. They would find her there in the strange man's bedroom after midnight—she, Millicent Bracegirdle, sister of the Dean of Easingstoke! Easingstoke! Visions of Easingstoke flashed through her alarmed mind. Visions of the news arriving, women whispering around tea-tables: "Have you heard, my dear? Really no one would have imagined! Her poor brother! He will, of course, have to resign, you know, my dear. Have a little more cream, my love."

Suddenly the awful horror was upon her.
There was a man asleep in her bed!

Would they put her in prison? She might be in the room for the purpose of stealing or she might be in the room for the purpose of breaking every one of the ten commandments. There was no explaining it away. She was a ruined woman, suddenly and irretrievably, unless she could open the door. The chimney? Should she climb up the chimney? But where would that lead to? And then she thought of the man pulling her down by the legs when she was already smothered in soot. Any moment he might wake up. She thought she heard the chambermaid going along the passage. If she had wanted to scream, she ought to have screamed before. The maid would know she had left the bathroom some minutes ago. Was she going to her room?

An abrupt and desperate plan formed in her mind. It was already getting on for one o'clock. The man was probably a quite harmless commercial traveller or business man. He would probably get up about seven or eight o'clock, dress quickly, and go out. She would hide under his bed until he went. Only a matter of a few hours. Men don't look under their beds, although she made a religious practice of doing so herself. When he went he would be sure to open the door all right. The handle would be lying on the floor as though it had dropped off in the night. He would probably ring for the chambermaid, or open it with a penknife. Men are so clever at those things. When he had gone she would creep out and steal back to her room, and then there would be no necessity to give any explanation to anyone. But heavens! what an experience! Once under the white frill of that bed, she would be safe until the morning. In daylight nothing seemed so terrifying. With feline precaution she went down on her hands and knees and crept towards the bed. What a lucky thing there was that broad white frill! She lifted it at the root of the bed and crept under. There was just sufficient depth to take her slim body. The floor was fortunately carpeted all over, but it seemed very close and dusty. Suppose she coughed or sneezed! Anything might happen. Of course, it would be much more difficult to explain her presence under the bed than to explain her presence just inside the door. She held her breath in suspense. No sound came from above, but under the frill it was difficult to hear anything. It was almost more nerve-racking than hearing everything—listening for signs and portents. This temporary escape, in any case, would give her time to regard the predicament detachedly. Up to the present she had not been able to focus the full significance of her action. She had, in truth, lost her head. She had been like a wild animal, consumed with the sole idea of escape—a mouse or a cat would do this kind of thing—take cover and lie low. If only it hadn't all happened *abroad*!

She tried to frame sentences of explanation in French, but French escaped her. And then they talked so rapidly, these people. They didn't listen. The situation was intolerable. Would she be able to endure a night of it? At present she was not altogether uncomfortable, only stuffy and—very, very frightened. But she had to face six or seven or eight hours of it, and perhaps even then discovery in the end! The minutes flashed by as she turned the matter over and over in her head. There was no solution. She began to wish she had screamed or awakened the man. She saw now that that would have been the wisest and most politic thing to do; but she had allowed ten minutes or a quarter of an hour to elapse from the moment when the chambermaid would know that she had left the bathroom. They would want an explanation of what she had been doing in the man's bedroom all that time. Why hadn't she screamed before?

She lifted the frill an inch or two and listened. She thought she heard the man breathing, but she couldn't be sure. In any case, it gave her more air. She became a little bolder, and thrust her face partly through the frill so that she could breathe freely. She tried to steady her nerves by concentrating on the fact that—well, there it was. She had done it. She must make the best of it. Perhaps it would be all right, after all.

"Of course, I shan't sleep," she kept on thinking. "I shan't be able to. In any case, it will be safer not to sleep. I must be on the watch."

She set her teeth and waited grimly. Now that she had made up her mind to see the thing through in this manner she felt a little calmer. She almost smiled as she reflected that there would certainly be something to tell the dear dean when she wrote to him to-morrow. How would he take it? Of course he would believe it—he had never doubted a single word that she had uttered in her life—but the story would sound so preposterous. In Easingstoke it would be almost impossible to imagine such an experience. She, Millicent Bracegirdle, spending a night under a strange man's bed in a foreign hotel! What would those women think? Fanny Shields and that garrulous old Mrs. Rusbridger? Perhaps—yes, perhaps it would be advisable to tell the dear dean to let the story go no farther. One could hardly expect Mrs. Rusbridger to not make implications—exaggerate. Oh, dear! what were they all doing now? They would all be asleep, everyone in Easingstoke. Her dear brother always retired at 10.15. He would be sleeping calmly and placidly the sleep of the just—breathing the dear sweet air of Sussex, not this—oh, it *was* stuffy! She felt a great desire to cough. She mustn't do that.

Yes, at 9.30 all the servants were summoned to the library. There was a short service—never more than fifteen minutes; her brother didn't believe in a great deal of ritual—

then at 10 o'clock cocoa for everyone. At 10.15 bed for everyone. The dear, sweet bedroom, with the narrow white bed, by the side of which she had knelt every night so long as she could remember—even in her dear mother's day—and said her prayers.

Prayers! Yes, that was a curious thing. This was the first night in her life experience when she had not said her prayers on retiring. The situation was certainly very peculiar—exceptional, one might call it. God would understand and forgive such a lapse. And yet, after all, why—what was to prevent her saying her prayers? Of course, she couldn't kneel in the proper devotional attitude, that would be a physical impossibility; nevertheless, perhaps her prayers might be just as efficacious—if they came from the heart.

So little Miss Bracegirdle curved her body and placed her hands in a devout attitude in front of her face, and quite inaudibly murmured her prayers under the strange man's bed.

At the end she added, fervently:

"Please God protect me from the dangers and perils of this night."

Then she lay silent and inert, strangely soothed by the effort of praying.

It began to get very uncomfortable, stuffy, but at the same time draughty, and the floor was getting harder every minute. She changed her position stealthily and controlled her desire to cough. Her heart was beating rapidly. Over and over again recurred the vivid impression of every little incident and argument that had occurred to her from the moment she left the bathroom. This must, of course, be the room next to her own. So confusing, with perhaps twenty bedrooms all exactly alike on one side of a passage—how was one to remember whether one's number was one hundred and fifteen or one hundred and sixteen? Her mind began to wander idly off into her schooldays. She was always very bad at figures. She disliked Euclid and all those subjects about angles and equations—so unimportant, not leading anywhere. History she liked, and botany, and reading about strange foreign lands, although she had always been too timid to visit them. And the lives of great people, *most* fascinating—Oliver Cromwell, Lord Beaconsfield, Lincoln, Grace Darling—*there* was a heroine for you—General Booth, a great, good man, even if a little vulgar. She remembered dear old Miss Trimmings talking about him one afternoon at the vicar of St. Bride's garden party. She was *so* amusing. She—*Good heavens!*

Almost unwittingly Millicent Bracegirdle had emitted a violent sneeze!

It was finished! For the second time that night she was conscious of her heart nearly stopping. For the second time that night she was so paralysed with fear that her mentality went to pieces. Now she would hear the man get out of bed. He would walk across to the door, switch on the light, and then lift up the frill. She could almost see that fierce moustachioed face glaring at her and growling something in French. Then, he would thrust out an arm and drag her out. And then? O God in Heaven! what then?

"I shall scream before he does it. Perhaps I had better scream now. If he drags me out he will clap his hand over my mouth. Perhaps chloroform—"

But somehow she could not scream. She was too frightened even for that. She lifted the frill and listened. Was he moving stealthily across the carpet? She thought— no, she couldn't be sure. Anything might be happening. He might strike her from above—with one of those heavy boots, perhaps. Nothing seemed to be happening, but the suspense was intolerable. She realised now that she hadn't the power to endure a night of it. Anything would be better than this—disgrace, imprisonment, even death. She would crawl out, wake the man, and try to explain as best she could.

She would switch on the light, cough, and say: "Monsieur!"

Then he would start up and stare at her.

Then she would say—what should she say?

"*Pardon, monsieur, mais je*—What on earth was the French for 'I have made a mistake'?

"*J'ai tort. C'est la chambre*—er—incorrect. *Voulez-vous*—er—?"

What was the French for "door-knob," "let me go"?

It didn't matter. She would turn on the light, cough, and trust to luck. If he got out of bed and came towards her, she would scream the hotel down.

The resolution formed, she crawled deliberately out at the foot of the bed. She scrambled hastily towards the door—a perilous journey. In a few seconds the room was flooded with light. She turned towards the bed, coughed, and cried out boldly:

"Monsieur!"

Then for the third time that night little Miss Bracegirdle's heart all but stopped. In this case the climax of the horror took longer to develop, but when it was reached it clouded the other two experiences into insignificance.

The man on the bed was dead!

She had never beheld death before, but one does not mistake death.

She stared at him, bewildered, and repeated almost in a whisper:

"Monsieur! Monsieur!"

Then she tip-toed towards the bed. The hair and moustache looked extraordinarily black in that grey, wax-like setting. The mouth was slightly open, and the face, which in life might have been vicious and sensual, looked incredibly peaceful and far away. It was as though she were regarding the features of a man across some fast passage of time, a being who had always been completely remote from mundane preoccupations.

When the full truth came home to her, little Miss Bracegirdle buried her face in her hands and murmured: "Poor fellow—poor fellow!"

For the moment her own position seemed an affair of small consequence. She was in the presence of something greater and more all-pervading. Almost instinctively she knelt by the bed and prayed.

For a few moments she seemed to be possessed by an extraordinary calmness and detachment. The burden of her hotel predicament was a gossamer trouble—a silly, trivial, almost comic episode, something that could be explained away.

But this man—he had lived his life, whatever it was like, and now he was in the presence of his Maker. What kind of man had he been?

Her meditations were broken by an abrupt sound. It was that of a pair of heavy boots being thrown down by the door outside. She started, thinking at first it was someone knocking or trying to get in. She heard the "boots," however, stumping away down the corridor, and the realisation stabbed her with the truth of her own position. She mustn't stop there. The necessity to get out was even more urgent.

To be found in a strange man's bedroom in the night is bad enough, but to be found in a dead man's bedroom was even worse. They would accuse her of murder, perhaps. Yes, that would be it—how could she possibly explain to these foreigners? Good God! they would hang her. No, guillotine her—that's what they do in France. They would chop her head off with a great steel knife. Merciful heavens! She envisaged herself standing blindfold, by a priest and an executioner in a red cap, like that man in the Dickens story. What was his name?—Sydney Carton, that was it. And before he went on the scaffold he said:

"It is a far, far better thing that I do than I have ever done—"

But no, she couldn't say that. It would be a far, far worse thing that she did. What about the dear dean; her sister-in-law arriving alone from Paraguay to-morrow; all her dear people and friends in Easingstoke; her darling Tony, the large grey tabby-cat? It was her duty not to have her head chopped off if it could possibly be avoided. She could do no good in the room. She could not recall the dead to life. Her only mission was to escape. Any minute people might arrive. The chambermaid, the boots, the manager, the gendarmes. Visions of gendarmes arriving armed with swords and notebooks vitalised her almost exhausted energies. She was a desperate woman. Fortunately now she had not to worry about the light. She sprang once more at the door and tried to force it open with her fingers. The result hurt her and gave her pause. If she was to escape she must *think*, and think intensely. She mustn't do anything rash and silly; she must just think and plan calmly.

She examined the lock carefully. There was no keyhole, but there was a slip-bolt, so that the hotel guest could lock the door on the inside, but it couldn't be locked on the outside. Oh, why didn't this poor dear dead man lock his door last night? Then this trouble could not have happened. She could see the end of the steel pin. It was about half an inch down the hole. If anyone was passing they must surely notice the handle sticking out too far the other side! She drew a hairpin out of her hair and tried to coax the pin back, but she only succeeded in pushing it a little farther in. She felt the colour leaving her face, and a strange feeling of faintness came over her.

She was fighting for her life; she mustn't give way. She darted round the room like an animal in a trap, her mind alert for the slightest crevice of escape. The window had no balcony, and there was a drop of five storeys to the street below. Dawn was breaking. Soon the activities of the hotel and the city would begin. The thing must be accomplished before then.

She went back once more and stared hard at the lock. She stared at the dead man's property, his razors and brushes and writing materials. He appeared to have a lot of writing materials, pens and pencils and rubber and sealing-wax. Sealing-wax!

Necessity is truly the mother of invention. It is in any case quite certain that Millicent Bracegirdle, who had never invented a thing in her life, would never have evolved the ingenious little device she did, had she not believed that her position was utterly desperate. For in the end this is what she did. She got together a box of matches, a candle, a bar of sealing-wax, and a hairpin. She made a little pool of hot sealing-wax, into which she dipped the end of the hairpin. Collecting a small blob on the end of it, she thrust it into the hole, and let it adhere to the end of the steel pin. At the seventh attempt she got the thing to move.

It took her just an hour and ten minutes to get that steel pin back into the room, and when at length it came far enough through for her to grip it with her finger-nails, she burst into tears through the sheer physical tenseness of the strain. Very, very carefully she pulled it through, and holding it firmly with her left hand she fixed the knob with her right, then slowly turned it.

The door opened!

The temptation to dash out into the corridor and scream with relief was almost irresistible, but she forebore. She listened. She peeped out. No one was about. With beating heart she went out, closing the door inaudibly; she crept like a little mouse to the room next door, stole in, and flung herself on the bed. Immediately she did so, it flashed through her mind that *she had left her sponge-bag and towel in the dead man's room!*

In looking back upon her experience she always considered that that second expedition was the worst of all. She might have let the sponge-bag and towel remain there, only that the towel—she never used hotel towels—had neatly inscribed in the corner "M. B."

With furtive caution she managed to retrace her steps. She re-entered the dead man's room, reclaimed her property, and returned to her own. When the mission was accomplished she was indeed well-nigh spent. She lay on her bed and groaned feebly. At last she fell into a fevered sleep.

It was eleven o'clock when she awoke, and no one had been to disturb her. The sun was shining, and the experiences of the night appeared a dubious nightmare. Surely she had dreamt it all?

With dread still burning in her heart she rang the bell. After a short interval of time the chambermaid appeared. The girl's eyes were bright with some uncontrollable excitement. No, she had not been dreaming. This girl had heard something.

"Will you bring me some tea, please?"

"Certainly, madame."

The maid drew back the curtains and fussed about the room. She was under a pledge of secrecy, but she could contain herself no longer. Suddenly she approached the bed and whispered, excitedly:

"Oh, madame, I am promised not to tell—but a terrible thing has happened! A man, a dead man, has been found in room one hundred and seventeen—a guest! Please not to say I tell you. But they have all been here—the gendarmes, the doctors, the inspectors. Oh, it is terrible—terrible!"

The little lady in the bed said nothing. There was indeed nothing to say. But Marie Louise Lancret was too full of emotional excitement to spare her.

"But the terrible thing is—Do you know who he was, madame? They say it is Boldhu, the man wanted for the murder of Jeanne Carreton in the barn at Vincennes. They say he strangled her, and then cut her up in pieces and hid her in two barrels, which he threw into the river. Oh, but he was a bad man, madame, a terrible bad man—and he died in the room next door. Suicide, they think; or was it an attack of the heart? Remorse; some shock, perhaps. Did you say a *café complet*, madame?"

"No, thank you, my dear—just a cup of tea—strong tea."

"*Parfaitement*, madame."

The girl retired, and a little later a waiter entered the room with tray of tea. She could never get over her surprise at this. It seemed so—well, indecorous for a man—although only a waiter—to enter a lady's bedroom. There was, no doubt, a great deal in what the dear dean said. They were certainly very peculiar, these French people—they had most peculiar notions. It was not the way they behaved at Easingstoke. She got farther under the sheets, but the waiter appeared quite indifferent to the situation. He put the tray down and retired.

When he had gone, she sat up and sipped her tea, which gradually warmed her. She was glad the sun was shining. She would have to get up soon. They said that her sister-in-law's boat was due to berth at one o'clock. That would give her time to dress comfortably, write to her brother, and then go down to the docks.

Poor man! So he had been a murderer, a man who cut up the bodies of his victims—and she had spent the night in his bedroom! They were certainly a most—how could she describe it?—people. Nevertheless she felt a little glad that at the end she had been there to kneel and pray by his bedside. Probably nobody else had ever done that. It was very difficult to judge people. Something at some time might have gone wrong. He might not have murdered the woman after all. People were often wrongly convicted. She herself. If the police had found her in that room at three o'clock that morning—It is that which takes place in the heart which counts. One learns and learns. Had she not learnt that one can pray just as effectively lying under a bed as kneeling beside it? Poor man!

She washed and dressed herself and walked calmly down to the writing-room. There was no evidence of excitement among the other hotel guests. Probably none of them knew about the tragedy except herself. She went to a writing-table, and after profound meditation wrote as follows:

"MY DEAR BROTHER,—I arrived late last night, after a very pleasant journey. Everyone was very kind and attentive, the manager was sitting up for me. I nearly lost my spectacles in the restaurant-car, but a kind old gentleman found them and returned them to me. There was a most amusing American child on the train. I will tell you about her on my return. The people are very pleasant, but the food is peculiar, nothing plain and wholesome. I am going down to meet Annie at one o'clock. How have you been keeping, my dear? I hope you have not had any further return of the bronchial attacks. Please tell Lizzie that I remembered in the train on the way here that that large stone jar of marmalade that Mrs. Hunt made is behind those empty tins on the top shelf of the cupboard next to the coach-house. I wonder whether Mrs. Buller was able to come to even-song after all? This is a nice hotel, but I think Annie and I will stay at the Grand to-night, as the bedrooms here are rather noisy. Well, my dear, nothing more till I return. Do take care of yourself.

"Your loving sister,
"MILLICENT."

Yes, she couldn't tell Peter about it, neither in the letter nor when she went back to him. It was her duty not to tell him. It would only distress him: she felt convinced of it. In this curious foreign atmosphere the thing appeared possible, but in Easingstoke the mere recounting of the fantastic situation would be positively indelicate. There was no escaping that broad general fact—she had spent a night in a strange man's bedroom. Whether he was a gentleman or a criminal, even whether he was dead or alive, did not seem to mitigate the jar upon her sensibilities, or, rather, it would not mitigate the jar upon the peculiarly sensitive relationship between her brother and herself. To say that she had been to the bathroom, the knob of the door-handle came off in her hand, she was too frightened to awaken the sleeper or scream, she got under the bed—well, it was all perfectly true. Peter would believe her, but—one simply could not conceive such a situation in Easingstoke deanery. It would create a curious little barrier between them, as though she had been dipped in some mysterious solution which alienated her. It was her duty not to tell.

She put on her hat and went out to post the letter. She distrusted an hotel letter-box. One never knew who handled these letters. It was not a proper official way of treating them. She walked to the head post-office in Bordeaux.

The sun was shining. It was very pleasant walking about amongst these queer, excitable people, so foreign and different looking—and the *cafés* already crowded with chattering men and women; and the flower stalls, and the strange odour of—what was it? salt? brine? charcoal? A military band was playing in the square—very gay and moving. It was all life, and movement, and bustle—thrilling rather.

"I spent a night in a strange man's bedroom."

Little Miss Bracegirdle hunched her shoulders, hummed to herself, and walked faster. She reached the post-office, and found the large metal plate with the slot for letters and R.F. stamped above it. Something official at last! Her face was a little flushed—was it the warmth of the day, or the contact of movement and life?—as she put her letter into the slot. After posting it she put her hand into the slot and flicked it round to see that there were no foreign contraptions to impede its safe delivery. No, the letter had dropped safely in. She sighed contentedly, and walked off in the direction of the docks to meet her sister-in-law from Paraguay.

3

Sanctuary in the School Library

In my boarding school it was almost impossible for a boy to have any kind of privacy.

Those in charge believed that if an adolescent was left alone for five minutes he would indulge in the most heinous and diabolical of activities, such as breaking windows, scribbling love notes to the baker's daughter (the only girl on the premises), decorating the gymnasium walls with obscene graffiti, or introducing stinging nettles into the beds of unpopular prefects.

'Don't leave them alone for a minute.' That was the headmaster's recipe for maintaining discipline, and most of the time it worked. Even the lavatories were without doors, so as to discourage too much time spent in the loo. We had to get used to other boys standing around, chatting to us while we attempted to defecate. The toilets flushed automatically, every five minutes. Sometimes they overflowed, and if our timing was awry, we had to make a dash for safety with our pants still down.

The lavatories, or 'bogs' as we called them, opened on to the hillside, and on one occasion I plonked myself down on a toilet seat only to find a large green snake coiled around the base of the toilet. It was probably a harmless grass snake, but I did not linger to find out.

Somehow, toilet paper was always in short supply, as was water, so most of us resorted to using pages from our exercise books, which only aggravated the jamming of the flush systems. Even the snakes took off when the toilets overflowed.

During my last two years at school an understanding senior master, Mr Knight, put me in charge of the school library, a capacious room a little distance from the classrooms and dormitories. It was called the Anderson Library, and I was the sole possessor of the keys to this little bit of heaven. Whenever I could escape from cricket nets (boring) or gymnastics (terrifying) or athletics practice (why run when you can walk?) I would sneak off to the library to explore the bookshelves. Making myself comfortable in the only armchair (the alternative was a hard bench), I would allow myself to be transported to another world through the pages of Somerset Maugham, Hugh Walpole, J.B. Priestley, P.G. Wodehouse, J.M. Barrie, Compton Mackenzie, Dornford Yates, John Buchan, John Masefield, and other successful novelists, poets and playwrights of the 1930s and 40s.

We still read some of them today. Others have been unfairly forgotten.

A novel that I really enjoyed was J.B. Priestley's *The Good Companions*, which followed the fortunes of a group of disparate characters who came together to form a small touring theatrical company. The story is full of good humour and good fellowship, qualities that are to be found in most of Priestley's work. There is a Dickensian roundness to his characters, as you will see from this extract in which the group comes together to choose a name for the company.

Priestley wrote many successful plays, and his love for the theatre comes through in this early novel as well as in one of his last works, *Lost Empires*. He was guide, philosopher and friend to many aspiring young writers. I have treasured the story of his own literary journey, *Margin Released*, for many years.

From *The Good Companions* (1929)
by J.B. Priestley

In Which They All Become "Good Companions"

At half-past seven that night, all our friends were assembled in the upstairs dining-room of The Royal Standard—with one exception. Miss Trant was not there. The Misses Dean and Longstaff, on being questioned, said they did not know why she was late. They had found very nice rooms for her next door but one to their own, and had left her there. She had, however, said something about a bath—"and you know what that means in these digs, my dear." Their various dears did know what it meant, and were relieved. "Though it wouldn't surprise *me* if something had happened to her, taken ill or lost her memory or all her money or something, right at the very crucial moment. That's the sort of thing that *would* happen, my dear." This was the dark verdict of Miss Stella Cavendish, otherwise Mrs. Joe Brundit, who was looking very festive and important and uncomfortable in her cerise, a dress that was rather too small for her now but had done good service some years ago during a season in "stock," when she had played the Duchess of Dorking and other great-lady parts, all with a song in the third act. But if Mrs. Joe, who had no illusions about the profession and was a great authority upon its ups-and-downs, especially the downs, was ready to be pessimistic about the non-appearance of their possible saviour, Miss Trant, this does not mean that she was out of tune with the festive evening. The Duchess of Dorking herself could not have surveyed and approved of the arrangements in better style. She hastened to congratulate her host, Mr. Jollifant: "Everything very nice, very tasteful, I'm sure," was her verdict.

"Mrs. Tidby—she's the proprietor—said the notice was too short," replied Inigo, "but that she'd do her best. And, she said, although she was not the one to say it, nobody in this town could do better. And she insisted upon telling me all about the annual dinner of the Rawsley and West Something-or-other Horticultural Society, which has been held here since 1898. So there!"

"All very nice, very tasteful," repeated Mrs. Joe, with bland complacency, casting her eye over the table, laid for ten. "Though nobody knows better than I do," she continued archly, "that so much depends on the orderer in these affairs. Get a good orderer and what happens?

Everything tasteful, nothing tawdry. How many can you trust to order? Now there's Mr. Brundit—Joe—he couldn't order, not to be satisfactory. He hasn't the manner. Joe's as gentle as a lamb and as strong as a lion, but he hasn't the manner. They'd say in a minute 'Anything'll do for *him*.' They *know*, these people, Mr. Jollifant. Now you're a gentleman. What does that mean? It means that it comes to you naturally, you're a born orderer."

"Oh, I don't know about that," Inigo protested, being the last person in the world to have any aristocratic pretensions. "I don't know that you can say that—"

"I do," said Mrs. Joe firmly, holding up her hand. "And when you've been as many years in the profession as I have, you'll know. I can tell it in a minute. I said to myself as soon as I met you: 'He's untidy; he may not have much money; he's ready for his little joke with everybody; but—he's a gentleman.' Oxford or Cambridge or Harrow, Mr. Jollifant?"

"Cambridge," said Inigo, staring.

"I knew. 'One of them,' I said to myself." She was very triumphant. "There's a *Stamp*. I've thought about it for George—that's our boy, you know. I said from the first, if that boy's bright—and you couldn't want a brighter—and if things will allow, he goes to one of those places. I don't care, I've told Joe more than once, whether it's Cambridge

College or Oxford College—I'm not one of your silly boat-race people—but to one of them, things allowing, he goes."

"Jolly good!" said Inigo heartily if a trifle absent-mindedly, for he was wondering when Miss Trant would come.

"*And* no stage. I've made up my mind about *that*. Joe says it would be nice to have him with us, and nobody knows that better than a mother, but what I say every time is that George must have his chance at something gentlemanly—a bank or estate agency. Concert singing I would *not* object to, but that depends on the Voice. So far, George has given no signs of having a Voice. If it comes, well and good. But no stage!"

"You're frightening me, Mrs. Brundit," said Inigo, smiling, "Don't forget I'm apparently just about to join the profession myself."

"Ah, that's your fun, Mr. Jollifant, I know," replied Mrs. Joe, turning her head a little to one side and raising her eyebrows. "Just a little experience for you, that's all. I believe you're a real musician."

"I'm not," said Inigo, laughing. "Anything but that. I'm just a piano-pounder. Writing's the only thing I'm really interested in."

"Writing? You have the look of an author too. Now if only I'd had the time, the things I could have written! The experience I *have* had, but never the time. What is it, Joe?" she enquired, for that gentleman was now standing at her elbow.

"It's quarter to eight, that's what it is," said Joe rather gloomily. "And Miss Trant's not here yet. I suppose she wasn't having a game with us, was she?"

"Oh, she wouldn't do a thing like that, Joe," cried his wife. "You could see at a glance she wasn't that sort. What I'm wondering is whether anything's happened to her. What if she lost her memory or was run over! Just when it seemed all right!"

"It'd be just our luck, Mag," said Joe, his face falling. They exchanged hollow stares, and for a moment or so Miss Stella Cavendish lost all resemblance to the Duchess of Dorking; she seemed to droop, to sag; she looked a tired woman who remembered she had a boy to support and that he was far away on Denmark Hill, that they had no money and some debts, that jobs were few and getting scarcer; a woman who had said good-bye to the easy elasticity of youth. Joe coughed. "It'll turn out all right, you'll see," he began gently.

Inigo turned away, for this was no place for him. He wandered round the room, keeping one eye on the door through which Miss Trant should enter at any moment. And all his other guests were keeping an eye on that door and were beginning to look anxious, though they kept up a little buzz of talk and pretended they did not care. Mr. Jimmy Nunn had cornered the old waiter in order to tell him that the whole dinner would be regarded by Mr. Nunn's digestive apparatus as poison and nothing less, and now he had Mrs. Tidby (who had a sister who was just the same) in his audience, and appeared to be presenting the two of them with a little act in which he took the part of a too sensitive and suspicious stomach. But even he watched the door all the time. Mr. Jerry Jerningham and Mr. Oakroyd, who had discovered that they could not talk to one another, looked about them and grinned rather vaguely, but kept most of their glances for the door. Mr. Morton Mitcham, who had unearthed a larger tie and an almost clean collar for the occasion, was playing Othello to the combined Desdemona of Miss Longstaff and Miss Dean, but when Inigo approached he broke off to ask the time. "Eight o'clock, is it?" he cried. "Well, well! I just wondered, you know." His eye went round to that door and then hastily retreated. "Well, as I was saying, Miss Longstaff, Miss Dean, I only once played Jo'burg in a thunderstorm, a real thunderstorm—"

Inigo began to feel anxious himself now. Suppose Miss Trant really didn't turn up! What a horrible fiasco this supper—as all the players called it—would be, with the show still in ruins, all their hopes scattered again! He went down the stairs, looked in several of the rooms there, then stood at the entrance for a minute or two, glancing up and down the square. When he returned he found the old waiter at the bottom of the stairs. "We're still one short," he explained. "Look here, couldn't you take some cocktails—gin and Italian or sherry and bitters or something—upstairs to those people, and ask them to help themselves." He had a cocktail himself at the bar, and no sooner had he swallowed it than he noticed a figure, an irresolute, hesitating figure, at the entrance. He rushed forward. It was Miss Trant.

"Come along, Miss Trant," he roared. "We're all waiting for you."

"I'm sorry," she stammered, still hesitating.

He stared curiously at her. What was the matter? "You know," he went on, in a lower voice, "those people upstairs—the poor old Dinky Doos—had begun to think you weren't turning up, and they were feeling very sick about it. They didn't say anything, which I thought jolly decent of them, but they were beginning to look a bit greenish, absolutely. You can't blame 'em, can you?"

"No, of course not," said Miss Trant. "And I'm sorry I've been so long. I—er—had to wait ages for a bath."

"Oh, I knew you'd come all right," said Inigo. His tone was cheerfully offhand, but he shot another curious glance at her as she came forward. "Baths, of course—well, that's asking for difficulties, isn't it?" he babbled, leading her to the stairs. "The old Rawsleyans have not quite grasped the idea of a bath yet. A panful—yes! Two panfuls—possible! But a bath, involving the contents of more than two pans or five kettles and the subsequent immersion of the human body—"

She stopped him at the foot of the stairs. "Listen, Mr. Jollifant. I feel I must tell somebody, and I think you'd understand. It's all very silly, of course—" she hesitated.

"Go on, Miss Trant," he said. "You must tell me now. As for it's being silly—well, we're all a bit silly, aren't we? I know I'm ridiculous, absolutely."

"I could have got here earlier," she began hastily, "only I suddenly discovered I wanted to—to run away. When I found myself alone again, I wondered why I had said I would go into this business. I don't know anything about it. I have some money, but not much really. And then it's all so different from the kind of life I have known. And when I thought about all this, I began to feel a bit sick about it and wanted to run away, to go back to my own kind of life, you know, to ordinary comfortable things—"

"Know! I should say I do," cried Inigo softly. "You get a crawly feeling somewhere at the bottom of your stomach, don't you?—you feel all cold and hollow inside—and then you curse yourself for having let yourself in for the thing—"

"That's it, exactly," she replied eagerly. "But surely you haven't felt like that?"

"Of course I have. This very night, for that matter! I feel like that whenever I try anything new, but I say— Down with it! You'd never do anything if you took any notice of that, would you? I mean, all this is as strange and absurd and unreal to me as it is to you, really, but I don't care."

"It's much worse, I think, for a woman. A young man can do anything for a time, it doesn't much matter—"

"And so can a woman, within reasonable limits. And this is well within 'em, isn't it?"

"I suppose so," she replied. "And if it *is* silly, I don't really mind. It's time I did something really silly. It's terrible being quiet and sensible all your life, isn't it?"

"Rather!" said Inigo, who had never tried it. "And I'm awfully glad you didn't run away, you know."

"And so am I. It was only a bit of me that wanted to, and it would have been mean and cowardly, you know, and I can't help thinking if I *had* gone, if I had sneaked back home—and I nearly did—I should have hated myself afterwards." They were climbing the stairs now. "I'm glad you understand, Mr. Jollifant." She drew a long breath, shook herself a little, then laughed. "I feel better now. Thank you."

"So do I, so don't thank me. And I'll do anything I can to help. I know nothing about this business, and I'm practically half-witted, except at times on paper—but there!"

They exchanged smiles at the top of the stairs, the smiles of two compatriots in a far and fantastic country. They were friends.

Inigo threw open the dining-room door. "Ladies and gentlemen," he roared. "Miss Trant."

A stir, a quick sigh, a buzz of welcome and a clapping of hands; and she stood for a moment or two in the doorway, looking at them all, half embarrassed, half delighted, no longer that familiar and only-to-be-expected figure, Miss Elizabeth Trant, who had stayed at the Old Hall so long that her youth had slipped by and all her bright looks been dimmed, but a mysterious Miss Trant who had popped up, come from nowhere, to save the show, and whose entrance lit up the room just as it lit up her face. As she stood there, she felt for a moment that she was a vivid and rather delightful person, one that even a busy Scots doctor might remember with pleasure. It was a moment well worth the whole six hundred pounds that had fallen to her last week out of the blue.

"And, if you'll allow me to say so, Miss Trant," said Mrs. Joe, otherwise Miss Stella Cavendish, sweeping forward impressively, "as pretty an entrance as one could wish for. It takes me back in a flash," she told the company, "to the big scene in *The Rose of Belgravia*."

"Take your seats, ladies and gentlemen," Inigo called out.

"Now where are we going to sit, Jollifant?" asked Mr. Morton Mitcham in his most dignified manner. "Quite like old times, Mrs. Brundit."

"I should say so," cried Miss Susie Dean. "The good old times when we all played the baby in *East Lynne*—perhaps. Well, I'm going to sit next to Mr. Oakroyd, because he's shy. Aren't ta, lad?"

"Noan too shy to gi' thee a bit of a slap, lass, if tha doesn't behave thysen," replied the delighted Mr. Oakroyd in his broadest accent. "Yond's a coughdrop," he announced to the room at large, and took his place beside her.

We have never heard that The Royal Standard in Rawsley is famous for its dinners, and as Mrs. Tidby herself pointed out more than once during the evening, the notice was short, so that it would be absurd to pretend that the dinner Inigo gave that night was an exquisite and memorable repast. Nevertheless, it seemed so to the whole ten of them. There were special reasons why it should. Miss Trant enjoyed it without noticing what she was eating, not because she was not interested in food but simply because she was still excited about herself and everybody else. Inigo enjoyed it both as a meal (for his interior still remembered Washbury Manor School) and as a lark that would inevitably beget other and wilder larks. Mr. Oakroyd was rather overawed and dubious at first; there were too many knives and forks for his peace of mind; but the company of the lively Miss Susie and the sight of a large glass of beer helped to reassure him, and soon he happily stared and grinned and ate like one who had suddenly found an appetite in fairyland. As for Mr. Morton Mitcham and the other players, they enjoyed it because it was a splendid novelty, eating at that hour, and something of a novelty, perhaps, eating at all, certainly eating steadily through four generous courses. Miss Susie Dean, who confessed that she had been living entirely on tea and bread-and-butter and brawn and apples for the past week, declared she had forgotten there was so much food in the world, and was promptly asked not to be vulgar by her colleague, Miss Longstaff, who was so determined to be ladylike that she carefully left a little of each course at the side of her plate, which was otherwise clean enough. Mr. Jerningham contrived to wear an expression of faint boredom throughout the dinner, but despatched it like an elegant wolf. Mr. Joe Brundit, who joined Mr. Oakroyd in his preference for a large glass of beer, demanded so many pieces of bread that he became an important figure in the waiter's reminiscences. But it was Mrs. Joe and Mr. Morton Mitcham who succeeded best in giving the dinner the air of being a prodigal feast. With them there seemed to be not four courses but fifty. The tomato soup, the mysterious little pieces of white fish, the boiled mutton, the blackberry and apple tart, were transformed by their histrionic gusto into a banquet of Lucullus, and they seemed to nod and smile at one another over the ruins of garnished peacocks' and nightingales' tongues. To see Mr. Mitcham fill Mrs. Joe's glass and then his own from the solitary bottle of Beaune was to catch a glimpse of the old mad bad days of the fine ladies and gentlemen who lived careless of the morrow, though the very tumbrils were rattling down the street. When they raised their glasses, the least you saw was a Viceroy or Governor-General of the old school and the Duchess of Dorking. It was a fine performance.

Even Mr. Jimmy Nunn contrived to enjoy the dinner in his own way. It was not the soup and fish and toast, to which he restricted himself, that he enjoyed, but his abstinence. As he groaned "Can't look at 'em—poison to me!", he did not seem to be refusing a little mutton and tart, but a gigantic host of dishes; waving away the very fat of the land. He referred to his stomach as if it were a haughty and eccentric guest he had brought with him. He crumbled his toast and sipped his whisky and soda ("Can't touch wine or beer") with a melancholy pride. He found time, however, to talk business with Miss Trant, who explained briefly and rather nervously her complete ignorance and her comparative poverty.

"If you've two or three hundred you're ready to play with," said Mr. Nunn, "that'll be more than enough. With any luck, you'll have it back in no time, and after that the profit begins, and you just lean back and count the boodle. I don't mind telling you, Miss Trant, if I'd half that, I'd be running the show myself. I wouldn't be sticking to the show if I didn't believe in it. I'm not like most of these boys and girls here. I could get another engagement—as good as this, if not better—tomorrow, 'cos I'm an old hand and well known in the profession. Matter of fact, I was getting twice their money, and might have got more if I'd stuck out for it. What are you people eating now? Blackberry pie? My word, you don't know your luck. I've nearly forgotten the taste of it." He sighed hugely.

"You're not missing so much, Mr. Nunn," Miss Trant whispered. "It's not very nice. The crust's too thick and stodgy."

"It looks like Heaven to me," he lamented. "But as I was saying, I believe in the show. We all do, and if we'd had the money, we'd have wanted nothing better than to have gone on ourselves, running it on a profit-sharing basis. You see what I mean?"

"Yes, of course I do," she exclaimed. "I'm not quite so ignorant as that, you know."

"Sorry, sorry! No offence meant, Miss Trant."

"And none taken! Isn't that the phrase?" She laughed, then added, lowering her voice: "As it is, I have to pay the company's debts—"

"You're not forced to," he put in. "You're not responsible for 'em. But it 'ud be better if you did. And then we could get all the props back, too."

"Certainly. Well, I pay them, and the salaries, of course, and I suppose the expenses." She was very business-like now, and was enjoying it.

"Yes, any expenses that crop up connected with the show," he replied, "such as railway fares, baggage fees, and all that, and anything that's wanted for production numbers, special costumes and effects, you know. But not costumes for individual numbers. We get them ourselves."

"And if there's any profit, it belongs to me?"

He groaned. "That is so but don't put it like that, Miss Trant. Spare a poor man who's had nothing but toast and mush and a bit of a fish he's never heard of. Don't think we're going to lose money for the rest of our lives. You make me feel like a Jonah. Put it this way. You take *all* the profits."

"That does sound better, doesn't it? And of course I should like a lot of profit, heaps and heaps of money, but somehow I can't believe there will be much."

He looked very solemn and thoughtful, screwing up his face until it seemed all shining nose and upper lip. It was absurd that he should look like that and yet talk business so sensibly. "I'll tell you what I'll do," he announced at last. "I was getting ten a week—I'll show you my agreement with Mildenhall tomorrow morning—"

"No, no," cried Miss Trant, "I don't want to see it. Go on, please."

"Now, if you want me to, I'll produce for you. I'm sure none of the boys and girls would object to that. I know the business all through."

"You mean that you would rehearse everything and be responsible for the programmes? That would be splendid, Mr. Nunn. Just what I wanted! Thank you."

"It's a pleasure, Miss Trant," he said solemnly. "And not only will I produce for you—and it means a lot of extra work—but I'll drop two pounds a week, making it eight. No, listen. Instead of that two pounds, I'll take fifteen per cent of your net profits. Now I've worked that out somewhere"—he brought out his notebook—"and you'll see it means—yes, here you are—it means that I'm not making up that two pounds unless you're making over thirteen a week net profit. Mind you, I'll tell you this—you won't make it at first. Don't expect it. We've got to pull the show together, and then again this is between seasons. Summer's over and it isn't winter. And another thing, we haven't got our dates right yet. We can't take Mildenhall's dates, at least not all of 'em, 'cos they're terrible. But that'll tell you whether I believe in the show or not."

"I'm sure you do," said Miss Trant warmly. "And I'm only too glad to accept that arrangement of yours. One thing I want to change, by the way, and that's the name. I don't like it, and besides I think we ought to start all over again."

"Not a bad name, you know," he replied thoughtfully. "And it's known. But that's up to you. We can easily find another, and as you say, make a fresh start. That might put more heart into the boys and girls. Very superstitious, us pro's, Miss Trant, and all sorts of little things bother us. Oh, and there's another thing. What about taking on these two new fellows? I've had a talk to 'em, and I advise it myself, but it's your business now, you know; you're the boss and you have 'em to pay."

"Mr. Jollifant we want, certainly," said the boss, flushing a little, "that is, if he's a good pianist. And I should think he is," she added, hopefully.

"Heard him before we came on here," said Mr. Nunn, "and he's first-class. He makes the last one we had seem like a piano-tuner in a fit. He's an amateur, but he's got real style. That other chap, Mitcham, swears by him, and he's got a lot of experience. I've heard of him before."

"He's a very queer-looking man," she said, dropping her voice. "He looks like somebody very grand and important who's all gone to seed."

Mr. Nunn shut one eye and curved a hand round his mouth. "One of the best banjoists in the profession, and a good conjurer," he whispered. "*And* one of the biggest liars. Wonderful! You have a talk to him. I don't say he hasn't seen a lot in his time, but to hear him talk you'd think he was the Wandering Jew's older brother. He's worth taking on just as a liar. Apart from that, though, he'll be worth his money all right. The conjuring'll come in as an extra, and he's just what we want for the band. We run a sort of little jazz band, you know, in the show, and a banjoist'll just make it up. I play the drums, and for a man who's forgotten what a square meal's like, I can rattle 'em a bit, I don't mind telling you." And he picked up a knife and fork and gave a little ratta-tat-tat on a plate. "Must use a knife and fork some time, eh?" he observed, at the end of the performance.

Perhaps the company thought it a signal for silence, or perhaps it was merely because the dinner was finished, but everybody stopped talking and looked rather expectantly towards Miss Trant and Mr. Nunn.

"Shall I talk to 'em?" asked Mr. Nunn.

"Yes, do," she replied. "But you ought to ask Mr. Jollifant. After all, he's the host. Do you mind, Mr. Jollifant" she said, turning to him, "if Mr. Nunn explains now what we're going to do?"

"That's the idea of the thing," cried Inigo. "To have a feed and then a grand pow-wow of the great chiefs. The idea, absolutely! Say on, Master Nunn."

That gentleman rose to his feet. "Ladies and gentleman," he began.

"Give him a hand," cried Miss Dean, who was in high spirits. And they gave him a hand, and so enthusiastically that the waiter, who was trying, though not trying very hard, to remove the crumbs from the table, was so startled that he retired precipitately. "And not so much of the 'Ladies and gentlemen,' Jimmy!" his friend Joe called out, to the disgust of Mrs. Joe, who was sitting erect, with her head a little to one side, her eyebrows well raised and her lips pursed up, as if all Dorking was looking at its Duchess.

"Boys and girls," said Mr. Nunn, "I'm not going to say much. You've had a good dinner; I haven't; and you ought to do the talking. I only want to say that Miss Trant here, as you know, is going to run the show—"

Applause for Miss Trant, in which the speaker himself joins heartily. The lady smiles confusedly, blushes, and for a moment or two wishes herself back at Hitherton.

"And we're going to turn it into the best little Concert Party on the road today," Jimmy continued. "We're lucky to have Miss Trant behind us. I think you'll think with me that Miss Trant'll think—half a minute, I'm getting too many 'thinks' in here, can't move for 'em. What I mean is, I hope Miss Trant will think soon she's been lucky too, to come across such a show." Cries of "Hear, hear!" and more applause. "You'll all be glad to know that we're completing the party at once. Mr. Morton Mitcham is joining us, and Mr. Mitcham, both on the banjo and with the cards, is an artiste of great talent and long and wide and—er—thick experience—"

"Four times round the world," that gentleman puts in, taking care to say it so that everybody will hear and yet contriving to appear as if he has merely spoken his thought aloud.

"Four times round the world," Mr. Nunn repeats, with a certain droll emphasis, "having played in Europe, Asia,

Africa, America, Australia, and the Isle o' Man. Am I right, sir?" Laughter and more applause. "Also, the place of the late pianist—"

"A nasty fumbler if there ever was one," remarks Mrs. Joe with great bitterness.

"Will be taken by Mr. Inigo Jollifant, who is new to the profession but is a first-class pianist as those of you who have heard him will testify. I ask you to remember too, boys and girls, that this is Mr. Jollifant's supper, though as far as I'm concerned, there hasn't been a supper. But you've all had one, and a good one."

More laughter and still more applause. Mr. Jollifant bows his acknowledgments, and seeing a welcoming smile on the face of Miss Susie Dean, he directs at her a specially companionable grin, only to discover that it is received with a haughty and disdainful stare. When he looks again he finds Miss Dean is pointedly drooping an eyelid at Miss Elsie Longstaff, and he comes to the conclusion that he has just been guyed by this dark and lively young lady.

Mr. Nunn has stopped, to confer in whispers with Miss Trant, who nods her head rapidly. The table is all attention.

"Look hare, what about—" begins Mr. Jerry Jerningham, but he gets no further, being fiercely requested by several of his colleagues to "shush."

"Now then," remarks Mr. Nunn, "there's just one or two points. As you boys and girls know, there's no reason why Miss Trant should pay any salaries at all until we start working again. But"—here Mr. Nunn takes a deep breath, and everybody looks relieved—"but she says she is willing to pay two weeks' money to all the old members of the party, that is, everybody but the two who've just joined. That means we're being paid for this week and last. And there'll be no cutting. Salaries the same as before." Here Mr. Nunn, who is too old a hand not to know when applause is coming, stops speaking. He is not disappointed.

There is, however, a dissentient. It is Mr. Jerry Jerningham, who now raises his beautiful head to voice a protest. "Look hare, Jaymy, thet's all raight about the two weeks' meney. Quaite generous, and all thet." (Here we must break in to say that though there is no more graceful and exquisite young man in the Midlands than Mr. Jerningham, his accent, a comparatively recent acquisition, unfortunately demands this kind of spelling. It is one thing to look at Mr. Jerningham, and quite another thing to listen to him. The thousands who have crowded in from Shaftesbury Avenue since then to see Jerry Jerningham will not recognise this accent, for the simple reason that he afterwards dropped it and then picked up another during his successful season on Broadway. Even the one we are trying to capture now was the third accent he had had since he quitted, at the age of seventeen, the outfitter's shop in Birmingham.) "But Ai cawn't agree to the same selery. Ai told Mildenhall Ai wasn't getting enough, considering the way mai ect was going, and he agreed—"

"Yes, you idiot," Miss Susie cries heatedly. "He'd agree to anything, considering-thet-he-wasn't-going-to-pay-you-anything-et-all. Fancy bringing that up! You're acting like a measly little Sheeny, Jerry Jerningham."

"Just maind your own business, Susie," he replies. "Nobody esked you to bett in. Ai'm talking to Miss Trarnt and Jaymy."

And neither Miss Trant nor Jimmy is looking with any great favour upon him. Both of them, indeed, are annoyed, and Miss Trant is quite ready to tell the beautiful youth that if he is not satisfied he can go. She glances with approval at the outspoken Susie. Jimmy is purpler than usual and might have been heard, a moment ago, muttering "Little blighter," but after a swift whispered aside to Miss Trant— "He's good, you know. Must try and keep him"—he now adopts a conciliatory attitude. Jerry has said that he is worth more than he is getting. All the boys and girls know that. They know that Jerry has been putting it across in great style, and will put it across in even greater style very soon. But the boys and girls will agree with him, Jimmy

Nunn, that in times like these an artiste cannot get what he is worth and is sometimes lucky to get anything at all. Things being what they were, Jerry must keep on at the old rate, like the rest of them. If Jerry's big chance came he could take it. Miss Trant was not going to bind any of them down. She was playing fair with them, and they would play fair with her. To all this the boys and girls gave a hearty assent, and Mr. Jerningham, whose chief desire had been to call attention to his own importance, gracefully signified that he would condescend to join them at the same salary as before.

"What's the programme then now, Jimmy?" Mr. Brundit calls out, in a voice that reminds everybody once again that many-brave-hearts-are-asleep-in-the-deep-so-beware. "Got to start again, haven't we?"

"I'm coming to that now, Joseph," Mr. Nunn informs him. "First thing, then—rehearsals. We've got to rehearse as if we'd never seen one another. Isn't that so? Well, what I propose is this—and, by the way, I ought to have said that Miss Trant wants me to produce for her and be the general big noise until she's got her hand in—we stop here and rehearse."

There are groans from the boys and girls, who have had quite enough of Rawsley. "A place," Mrs. Joe observed, "that would take the blood out of a stone."

"That's all right. I know how you feel about it," Jimmy continues, "and I'm all for the first train out myself. But one thing you've got to remember. We can't have a Treasury tomorrow—a little sub might be managed, that's all—because Miss Trant's got to have time to get her money through. It'll be Saturday or Monday before the ghost walks. And we'll have to settle up before we go. The other thing is, we've got the use of the hall this week and can rehearse there, and might get the use of it in the mornings and afternoons for a pound or two or for nothing if we stick out for it when we pay up, for part of next week. The date for next week's already cancelled. We could get a two or three night stand between here and Sandybay, where we're going the week after, and try out the new show then. How's that? Oh, and another thing! We're going to change the name. Miss Trant doesn't like the one we've got and anyhow we ought to start afresh with another one—change the luck, y'know. Now, any ideas for a new name?"

Several of them suggest names, all of which, it is triumphantly proved, have been used before—"for ages, my dear, simply ages." Mr. Joe Brundit (it is impossible to call him Courtney at such a moment) quite solemnly proposes they should call themselves "The Mugs"—he calls this "catchy"—but is at once howled down. His wife brings out "The Duennas," admits that she has forgotten what a Duenna is, but points out that it has a fine operatic flavour. Summarily rejected. Mr. Morton Mitcham is heard remarking that "The Wallahs," the name of a troupe he coached at either Simla or Bangalore in Nought Five, might be revived. His suggestion not meeting with approval, he rises—looking, as Miss Dean observes, as if he is never going to stop—and after clearing his throat in a very impressive manner and lowering his gigantic eyebrows at those persons who are still talking, he says: "Miss Trant, ladies and gentlemen. While we are cudgelling our brains to find a suitable name for the show, I propose—as I have proposed on many occasions in many different parts of the world before today—that we should—er—exhibit our appreciation, that is, display our grateful thanks, to our host, my friend, and your new colleague, Mr. Inigo Jollifant. Mr. Jollifant and I have already had some—er—interesting experiences together, have gone through bad times and good times. We met—er—in extraordinary circumstances—as Mr. Jollifant will remember." He paused, and everybody stared at Inigo, who began to feel that he and Mitcham must really have wandered across whole continents together. There was something compelling about Mitcham's epical imagination. "And on that occasion, after a very short acquaintance, I told him he

was a trouper, a good trouper. Those of you who are not—
er—familiar with the Transatlantic Stage may not know
the term. It is one, I may say, of the highest praise. I knew
then that our friend, Mr. Jollifant, was a good trouper. He
has proved to all of you, ladies and gentlemen, tonight that
he is a good trouper. And I propose that we all show our
appreciation. Mr. Jollifant!"

And they all do show their appreciation. Mr. Jollifant is
called upon to reply. He grins, thrusts back his lock of hair,
grins again, and puts back the lock in its usual place. It is, he
stammers, awfully good of everybody. He is overwhelmed,
absolutely. He is not sure what a trouper is. His knowledge
of America is very small and is chiefly derived from a study
of *Huckleberry Finn*.

Here he is interrupted by no less a person than
Miss Trant, with whom *Huckleberry Finn* is a very old
favourite indeed, and who now boldly claps her hands and
cries "Isn't it glorious?"

"Isn't it!" Inigo replies, and looks for a moment as if he
is about to sit down and spend the next half-hour talking
to Miss Trant about that masterpiece. Then he remembers
he is making a speech. "As I said before, I'm not very sure
what a trouper is, except that he or she is one who—er—
troupes. Therefore, I don't exactly know what constitutes a
good trouper. But if it means being a good companion, or

trying to be a good companion, then I'm proud to be called one, absolutely. Somehow"—he was in earnest now, saying for once something that was very real and important, felt in the heart, and not being, in spite of all his easy chatter, one of that rapidly increasing horde of glib self-confessors, he could only stammer it out—"somehow—there isn't too much—er—good companionship left—is there? I mean—people don't sort of—pull together now much, do they? Everybody's—well, not everybody, but a lot of people—are out for a good time—and that's all right, of course; I'm all for it; the more the merrier, so to speak—but it's nearly always their own good time and nobody else's they're out after, isn't it? An awful lot of hard nuts about now, somehow—and only soft in the wrong places. Well, of course, I'm not any better than anybody else, bit worse, I dare say, but I'd like one or two people to say I was a good companion. That's one of the things that's attracted me about this what's it—concert party; a good crowd sticking together. That's where the fun really comes in, isn't it? Look here, I'm making an awful mess of this, y'know. I can gas but I can't really talk—but"—he ends with a sudden burst—"I could write it, and I will do before long. Thanks very much."

"Listen, everybody," Miss Trant calls out at once. "Mr. Jollifant has given me the name. I'm sure it's never been used before. We'll call ourselves *The Good Companions*. What do you think of that?" She is very excited now.

The Good Companions. They are all turning it over and over, tasting it.

Inigo approves of it at once and with enthusiasm.

"I like it too," cries Miss Susie Dean. "It's original, and it does mean something, not like the ridiculous 'Dinky Doos.' That always made me feel as if I was something between a scented cigarette and one of those sixpenny packets of dye that Elsie here's always using. I like the sound of this new name. I don't know how it will look on the bills, though," she concludes doubtfully.

"I do," Mrs. Joe announces in a very deep and gloomy voice. "It will look rotten on the bills."

"I agree. Not enough *dash* about it, if you ask me," says Miss Elsie Longstaff, who is all for dash.

"Too haybrow, Miss Trarnt," is Mr. Jerningham's comment.

Mr. Nunn closes one eye over it, then the other, and finally declares it is a bit on the stiff side and won't space well on the bills—but—it is out of the common and will do. Mr. Mitcham comes down on the same side with all the weight of his experience. The combined enthusiasm of Miss Trant and Inigo is more than a match for the vague doubts and fears of the others.

"There it is then," Miss Trant calls out in her clear voice. "We'll call ourselves *The Good Companions*."

Here Mr. Mitcham has an inspiration. After saying to Inigo "Now this is *mine*," he rises to his full height and thunders: "Waiter. Where are you, waiter? Ah, there you are. Waiter, I want a bottle of port."

"Now what kind would you like, sir?" the waiter enquires, quite anxiously, as if the cellar is stocked with all manner of ports and he is gravely concerned lest the gentleman should not have exactly the right one.

"Oh, something drinkable. What have you got?"

"Well, we've the Tawny at three-and-nine the bottle, and we've the Old and Crusted at four-and-six."

"Than bring a bottle of the Old and Crusted," and Mr. Mitcham gives such richness to his vowel sounds that already the wine seems twice as old and crusted as it was before. "And glasses round," he continues, "as quick as you can." After almost chasing the waiter out of the room with his eyebrows, Mr. Mitcham sits down with the air of a man who not only knows a good wine but also knows how to order a good wine.

"Now he'd make a wonderful feed if I can get him going. Got just the style," Mr. Nunn whispers to his neighbour, Miss Trant. "And I've got a sketch or two that he can walk away with, right from the word 'go.'"

The Old and Crusted has arrived and so have the glasses. "I'm going to give you a toast in a minute," says Mr. Mitcham, "so fill up, everybody." When they are ready, he lifts his glass and cries in a voice of such majesty that it brings Mrs. Tidby upstairs from the bar: "My friends, I give you '*The Good Companions*.' Long life and good luck to 'em."

"I'll drink this," Mr. Nunn declares, "if it kills me." And down goes his Old and Crusted with the rest.

"*The Good Companions!*"

Mrs. Tidby, nodding and smiling at the door, is invited in to drink the health of the new show, which she does with great gusto, smacking her lips over the Old and Crusted to indicate perhaps that there is nothing wrong with it.

It is now Mr. Oakroyd's turn. Up to now he has been quiet because he is a diffident man and rather out of his element. All the others are members of the party, but he is only a guest. There had been some talk outside that teaplace about him doing something, but nothing has been said since and he is not one to push himself in where he isn't wanted. Tomorrow he will be wandering on his way again, but he has enjoyed tonight, and must say something to them all before they separate. So now he raises the large glass, which still has an inch of beer in it, and cries to them all: "Well, I'm nobbut one o' t'audience, as you might say. But this is my bit. May you mak' good companions o' t'fowk as comes to see and hear you, and nivver look back." And down went the inch of beer.

"Thank you, Mr. Oakroyd," Miss Trant calls out before anybody else could reply. And then she begins speaking in a low voice to Mr. Nunn.

Miss Dean, who seems to regard Mr. Oakroyd as her protégé, is delighted. "Isn't he sweet?" she cries across the table, and turns to look at him, with her head tilted to one side. "You *are* sweet, you know, Mr. Oakroyd, aren't you?" And her glance suggests that he is about six inches high and covered with pink icing.

But Mr. Oakroyd is now summoned to the end of the table, where Miss Trant and Mr. Nunn are in conference. He exchanges places with Inigo, who seems rather pleased to find himself next to Miss Dean, still smiling and altogether very attractive.

"Now listen, Mr. Oakroyd," Miss Trant is saying. "Mr. Nunn says that a handyman like you would be very useful to us—"

"Stage carpenter, props and baggage man, lights, doorman where needed, bill-poster where needed," Mr. Nunn rattles off this list with an easy air. "And of course any odd jobs."

"Ay." Mr. Oakroyd rubs his chin. You would not suppose for a moment that he is delighted. "Well, I know nowt about the-aters, nowt at all but what you can see from t'gallery. I could pick a deal up, I dare say. I can do owt I want to do wi' my hands as a rule. Is it summat you want doing or a reg'lar job?"

"We want you to travel round with us, Mr. Oakroyd, as our handyman," Miss Trant explained. "And I'm sure you'd soon learn anything you didn't know that had to be known. About lights, for instance."

A grin slowly broadens over Mr. Oakroyd's face. "One o' t'*Good Companions*, eh? By gow, I'll have a do at it, I will an' all."

"And Mr. Nunn suggests three pounds a week—"

"Plus train fares and any extra expenses," Mr. Nunn adds. "And good money too. Coming in regularly—very good money."

"Would that be all right, Mr. Oakroyd?"

"Eh, I should think so, Miss. Three pund i' t'week and nobbut mysen to keep! Nivver thowt I'd end up as a the-ater chap! This beats t'band, this does." And he chuckles away.

"That's all right, then, is it? Will you come down to the Assembly Rooms in the morning, Mr. Oakroyd?"

"Nobbut say t'word," says Mr. Oakroyd earnestly, "and I'll be down at half-past six wi' my tools."

"Half-past six!" Mr. Nunn gives a capital imitation of a gentleman who has just received a severe blow at the back of the head. "There isn't such a time, not in the morning—never heard of it—don't believe it exists. Nay, lad. Half-past ten's our time."

"Day's half ower i' Bruddersford by then. Happen you know Bruddersford, Mr. Nunn?"

"I do know Bruddersford," Mr. Nunn replies in tragic accents, "Everybody knows it, except the lucky ones. Ask Susie there about it, She calls it 'Shuddersford.' It's generally known to the profession though as 'The Comedian's Grave!'"

"Eh, whativver for?" enquires Mr. Oakroyd, his face quite wooden. "I've heard tell of 'em calling it t'place where they hammer screws. You hear all sorts, don't you, Mr. Nunn?" And he leans back in his chair and calmly stares at the ceiling.

Miss Trant, after looking at the pair of them, laughs a little, and Mr. Nunn laughs too, and then Mr. Oakroyd begins to chuckle again, "They're a bit o' good company, this lot," he tells himself, and when he remembers that he is not leaving them tomorrow but is going to travel all over the place and do odd jobs and have three pounds a week, he feels ready to burst.

Now they are calling "Miss Trant. Spee-eech, Miss Trant. Spee-eech." At first she shakes her head, but the boys and girls will take no refusal, as Mr. Nunn is careful to point out to her.

"I haven't anything to say at all, you know," she tells them, "except that I'm sure we shall all get on very well together. You must forgive me if I make mistakes or say anything silly, because, as you know, I don't really understand this business. I haven't even seen you on the stage, which is rather absurd, isn't it? But I'm sure you're all very clever and work very hard and—and—tomorrow and afterwards when you're Good Companions you'll be cleverer still and work harder." Laughter and applause. "And now I'm going to bed. Yes, I am. I've had an awfully long and exciting day—it seems to have lasted about a week—and now I'm tired."

"Oh, don't go, Miss Trant," Susie implores.

"Why not?"

"Well, if you go, I shall feel I ought to go too, and though I'm tired ish too, I hate to think I'm missing anything."

"I'm ready to go, Susie," Miss Longstaff tells her.

"Oh, all right then," cries Susie. "I suppose all us feemiles had better trot off together, and leave the men to stay here until they're kicked out. Can't you just see them here when we've gone—going yaw-yaw-yaw and haw-haw-haw and all of 'em nearly dying of conceit? I do think men are ridiculous," she concludes, putting her nose in the air.

"You stick fast to that opinion of the men, my dear," Mrs. Joe tells her, "and you might have a chance of getting to the top of the tree." And with that, the good lady rises, informs her husband that he can have another glass and no more, and stay just half an hour, then departs with the other three members of her sex.

And the men, sitting down again with that fine careless ease that comes when the women go, do have another and do yaw-yaw-yaw and haw-haw-haw, and while they are doing that, Inigo discovers that Jerry Jerningham, with his good looks and grace and weird accent, his determination to top the bill and have his name in electric lights before long or perish, his grave and almost ascetic devotion to his flimsy little art, is altogether an astonishing person; and Mr. Oakroyd discovers that Joe, whom he recognises at once as a man after his own heart, is not only partial to a pipe of *Old Salt* (to say nothing of a glass of beer) but is also a fellow enthusiast in the matter of football, at which little George will very soon distinguish himself— and surprise some of 'em, it appears—at Denmark Hill; and Jimmy Nunn and Morton Mitcham discover that they remember any number of "pros" who have got there or dropped out or lifted an elbow too often or gone into management or taken a nice little pub somewhere. Mrs. Tidby reappears, to hope everything was to their liking and to point out once again that the notice was short, and then to glance significantly at the clock. The old waiter yawns, pushes a few glasses about in an aimless fashion, returns with change on a little wet tray, smiles vaguely when told to keep it, then yawns again. They troop out into the deserted streets and stop a minute, with a faint shrinking sense of irony, to look up at the thinning clouds and the mild stars beyond. "You going my way? Right you are. Good night, boys. Good night, ol' man. Goo' night."

4

A Daring Young Man on a Bedpan

Another hospital bed; but this time in the general ward of the Hampstead General Hospital.

I had been in London for about six months, living on my own in a small bed-sitting room on Haverstock Hill. My Jewish landlady would give me an early breakfast, and then I'd be off on a tube train to the Tottenham Court Road station. From there it was a short walk to the Photax office on Charlotte Street, where I worked as an accounts clerk. It was a tedious, unexciting job, but it brought me five pounds a week, just enough for my room and breakfast, with a little left over for meals and the occasional visit to a cinema. At night I worked on my novel.

But I wasn't looking after myself. In the lunch breaks I would stroll across to a snack bar on Tottenham Court Road, consume baked beans on toast, and occasionally a chocolate Mars Bar, and that would be lunch. Sometimes a fellow clerk, Ken Murrell, would share his Marmite sandwiches with me. In the evening I would eat in a cheap ABC restaurant or station café. After a few months of these irregular meals I found that my vision was getting affected.

I was seeing more than spots, I was seeing dark clouds moving about before my right eye.

I went to an eye specialist (free, on the National Health Service) and he had me admitted to Hampstead General, where I was given a series of tests. I was told that I had a rare condition, Eales' Disease (nothing to do with consuming eels), brought on partly by dysentery (which I'd carried with me from India) and partly by malnutrition. I was given Emetine injections for the dysentery, cortisone injections in the eye (cortisone was a new steroid then, and they were trying it for everything), and second helpings of Irish stew or good old English shepherd's pie for my malnutrition. Sometimes, as a special treat, a bottle of Guinness—a light ale—would be provided with my lunch. All on the National Health Service!

I couldn't complain. And didn't.

There was some improvement in my vision (although it never cleared up completely), and after a few days a trolley filled with books appeared at my bedside, wheeled in by a beautiful nurse who looked like Jennifer Jones, a film star of that era. I lingered over the books, hoping the nurse would stay; but she had other things to do, and left me to explore the bookshelf.

In all, I was in the hospital for a month. In that time I got through some fifteen to twenty books. Among other writers that I enjoyed during my sojourn in the general ward was Josephine Tey, who had written three or four detective novels—*The Daughter of Time*, *Miss Pym Disposes*, *A Shilling for Candles*. Unfortunately she died quite young, otherwise I am sure she would have gone on to rival such well-established writers of detective fiction as Margery Allingham, Ngaio Marsh, and Dorothy L. Sayers

In *The Daughter of Time*, the detective (bed-ridden as I was) sets out to prove that King Richard the Third was innocent of the murder of the young princes in the Tower. This he does with the help of a visiting student and without leaving his hospital bed. There was something original, different, about all Josephine Tey's novels. Aficionados of the detective story should search for her books.

However the works I most enjoyed were the stories and novels of William Saroyan, whose outlook on life suited my own mood at the time.

Saroyan had made his name with a play, *The Time of Your Life*, which had earned him a Pulitzer prize. He had also written the story and screenplay for a wartime Hollywood film, *The Human Comedy*, which I had seen while still at school. Now I was able to read *My Name is Aram*, probably his best book, a collection of stories about an immigrant Armenian boy growing up in Fresno, California. They were funny, whimsical, optimistic, and in many ways they reminded me of my own boyhood in Delhi, Simla and Dehradun. His collection of essays, *The Daring Young Man on the Flying Trapeze*, was even more exciting, appealing to my own assertion of individuality. He was 'different'—a forerunner of the Beat Generation, and I could identify with his unique brand of individualism. The chapter that I include here will give you an idea of what I mean.

*

For the first few days in Hampstead General I was confined to my bed, hence the reference to the bedpan in the title of this chapter. As a result of my medications I had to make frequent use of the bedpan, with the result that some of the other patients gave me the title of 'Bedpan Superman'. Typical British humour, of course; and the only time in my life that I have been compared to Superman.

From *The Daring Young Man on the*
Flying Trapeze (1935)
by William Saroyan

Myself upon the Earth

A beginning is always difficult, for it is no simple matter to choose from language the one bright word which shall live forever; and every articulation of the solitary man is but a single word. Every poem, story, novel and essay, just as every dream is a word from that language we have not yet translated, that vast unspoken wisdom of night, that grammarless, lawless vocabulary of eternity. The earth is vast. And with the earth all things are vast, the skyscraper and the blade of grass. The eye will magnify if the mind and soul will allow. And the mind may destroy time, brother of death, and brother, let us remember, of life as well. Vastest of all is the ego, the germ of humanity, from which is born God and the universe, heaven and hell, the earth, the face of man, my face and your face; our eyes. For myself, I say with piety, rejoice.

I am a young man in an old city. It is morning and I am in a small room. I am standing over a bundle of yellow writing paper, the only sort of paper I can afford, the kind that sells at the rate of one hundred and seventy sheets for ten cents. All this paper is bare of language, clean and perfect, and I am a young writer about to begin my work. It is Monday . . . September 25, 1933 . . . how glorious it is to be alive, to be still living. (I am an old man; I have walked along many streets, through many cities, through many days and many nights. And now I have come home to myself. Over me, on the wall of this small, disordered room, is the photograph of my dead father, and I have come up from the earth with his face and his eyes and I am writing in English what he would have written in our native tongue. And we are the same man, one dead and one alive.) Furiously I am smoking a cigarette, for the moment is one of great importance to me, and therefore of great importance to everyone. I am about to place language, my language, upon a clean sheet of paper, and I am trembling. It is so much of a responsibility to be a user of words. I do not want to say the wrong thing. I do not want to be clever. I am horribly afraid of this. I have never been clever in life, and now that I have come to a labour even more magnificent than living itself, I do not want to utter a single false word. For months I have been telling myself, "You must be humble. Above all things, you must be humble." I am determined not to lose my character.

I am a story-teller, and I have but a single story, the story of man on earth. I want to tell this simple story in my own way, forgetting the rules of rhetoric, the tricks of composition. I have something to say and I do not wish to speak like Balzac. I am not an artist; I do not really believe in civilization. I am not at all enthusiastic about progress. When a great bridge is built I do not cheer, and when airplanes cross the Atlantic I do not think, "What a marvellous age this is!" I am not interested in the destiny of nations, and history bores me. What do they mean by history, those who write it and believe in it? How has it happened that man, that humble and lovable creature, has been exploited for the purpose of monstrous documents? How has it happened that his solitude has been destroyed, his godliness herded into a hideous riot of murder and destruction? And I do not believe in commerce. I regard all machinery as junk, the adding-machine, the automobile, the railway engine, the airplane, yes, and the bicycle. I do not believe in transportation, in going places with the body, and I would like to know where anyone has ever gone. Have you ever left yourself? Is any journey so vast and interesting as the journey of the mind through life? Is the end of any journey so beautiful as death?

I am interested only in man. Life I love, and before death I am humble. I cannot fear death because it is purely physical. Is it not true that today both I and my father are living, and that in my flesh is assembled all the past of man? But I despise violence and I hate bitterly those who perpetrate and practise it. The injury of a living man's small finger I regard as infinitely more disastrous and ghastly than his natural death. And when multitudes of men are hurt to death in wars I am driven to a grief which borders on insanity. I become impotent with rage. My only weapon is language, and while I know it is stronger than machine-guns, I despair because I cannot single-handed annihilate the notion of destruction which propagandists awaken in men. I myself, however, am a propagandist, and in this very story I am trying to restore man to his natural dignity and gentleness. I want to restore man to himself. I want to send him from the mob to his own body and mind. I want to lift him from the nightmare of history to the calm dream of his own soul, the true chronicle of his kind. I want him to be himself. It is proper to herd only cattle. When the spirit of a single man is taken from him and he is made a member of a mob, the body of God suffers a ghastly pain, and therefore the act is a blasphemy.

I am opposed to mediocrity. If a man is an honest idiot, I can love him, but I cannot love a dishonest genius. All my life I have laughed at rules and mocked traditions, styles and mannerisms. How can a rule be applied to such a wonderful invention as man? Every life is a contradiction, a new truth, a new miracle, and even frauds are interesting. I am not a philosopher and I do not believe in philosophies; the word itself I look upon with suspicion. I believe in the right of man to contradict himself. For instance, did I not say that I look upon machinery as junk, and yet do I not worship the typewriter? Is it not the dearest possession I own?

And now I am coming to the little story I set out to tell. It is about myself and my typewriter, and it is perhaps a trivial story. You can turn to any of the national five-cent magazines and find much more artful stories, stories of love and passion and despair and ecstasy, stories about men called Elmer Fowler, Wilfred Diggens, and women called Florence Farwell, Agatha Hume, and so on.

If you turn to these magazines, you will find any number of perfect stories, full of plot, atmosphere, mood, style, character, and all those other things a good story is supposed to have, just as good mayonnaise is supposed to have so much pure olive oil, so much cream, and so much whipping. (Please do not imagine that I have forgotten myself and that I am trying to be clever. I am not laughing at these stories. I am not laughing at the people who read them. These works of prose and the men and women and children who read them constitute one of the most touching documents of our time, just as the motion pictures of Hollywood and those who spend the greatest portion of their secret lives watching them constitute one of the finest sources of material for the honest novelist. Invariably, let me explain, when I visit the theatre, and it is rarely that I have the price of admission, I am profoundly moved by the flood of emotion which surges from the crowd, and newsreels have always brought hot tears from my eyes. I cannot see floods, fires, tornadoes, train wrecks, riots, wars and the faces of politicians without weeping. Even the tribulations of Mickey Mouse make my heart bleed, for I know that he, artificial as he may be, is actually a symbol of man.) Therefore, do not misunderstand me. I am not a satirist. There is actually nothing to satirize, and everything pompous or fraudulent contains its own mockery. I wish to point out merely that I am a writer, a story-teller. I go on writing as if all the periodicals in the country were clamouring for my work, offering me vast sums of money for anything I might choose to say. I sit in my room smoking one cigarette after another, writing this story of mine, which I know will never be able to meet the stiff competition of my more artful and talented contemporaries. Is it not strange? And why should I, a story-teller, be so attached to my typewriter? What earthly good is it to me? And what satisfaction do I get from writing stories?

Well, that is the story. Still, I do not want anyone to suppose that I am complaining. I do not want anyone to feel that I am a hero of some sort, or, on the other hand, that I am a sentimentalist. I am actually neither of these things. I have no objection to *The Saturday Evening Post*, and I do not believe the editor of *Scribner's* is a fool because he will not publish my tales. I know precisely what every magazine in the country wants. I know the sort of material *Secret Stories* is seeking, and the sort *The American Mercury* prefers, and the sort preferred by the literary journals like *Hound & Horn*, and all the rest. I read all magazines and I know what sort of stuff will sell. Still, I am seldom published and poor. Is it that I cannot write the sort of stuff for which money is paid? I assure you that it is not. I can write any sort of story you can think of. If Edgar Rice Burroughs were to die this morning, I could go on writing about Tarzan and the Apes. Or, if I felt inclined, I could write like John Dos Passos or William Faulkner or James Joyce. (And so could you, for that matter.)

But I have said that I want to preserve my identity. Well, I mean it. If in doing this it is essential for me to remain unpublished, I am satisfied. I do not believe in fame. It is a form of fraudulence, and any famous man will tell you so. Any honest man, at any rate. How can one living man possibly be greater than another? And what difference does it make if one man writes great novels which are printed and another writes great novels which are not? What has the printing of novels to do with their greatness? What has money or the lack of it to do with the character of a man?

But I will confess that you've got to be proud and religious to be the sort of writer that I am. You've got to have an astounding amount of strength. And it takes years and years to become the sort of writer that I am, sometimes centuries. I wouldn't advise any young man with a talent for words to try to write the way I do. I would suggest that he study Theodore Dreiser or Sinclair Lewis. I would suggest even that, rather than attempt my method, he follow in the footsteps of O. Henry or the contributors to *The Woman's Home Companion*. Because, briefly, I am not a writer at all. I have been laughing at the rules of writing ever since I started to write, ten, maybe fifteen, years ago. I am simply a young man. I write because there is nothing more civilized or decent for me to do.

Do you know that I do not believe there is really such a thing as a poem-form, a story-form or a novel-form? I believe there is man only. The rest is trickery. I am trying to carry over into this story of mine the man that I am. And as much of my earth as I am able. I want more than anything else to be honest and fearless in my own way. Do you think I could not, if I chose, omit the remark I made about Dos Passos and Faulkner and Joyce, a remark which is both ridiculous and dangerous? Why, if someone were to say to me, "All right, you say you can write like Faulkner, well, then, let's see you do it." If someone were to say this to me, I would be positively stumped and I would have to admit timidly that I couldn't do the trick. Nevertheless, I make the statement and let it stand. And what is more, no one can prove that I am cracked; I could make the finest alienist in Vienna seem a raving maniac to his own disciples, or if I did not prefer this course, I could act as dull and stupid and sane as a Judge of the Supreme Court. Didn't I say that in my flesh is gathered all the past of man? And surely there have been dolts in that past.

I do not know, but there may be a law of some sort against this kind of writing. It may be a misdemeanour. I hope so. It is impossible for me to smash a fly which has tickled my nose, or to step on an ant, or to hurt the feelings of any man, idiot or genius, but I cannot resist the temptation to mock any law which is designed to hamper the spirit of man. It is essential for me to stick pins in pompous balloons. I love to make small explosions with the inflated bags of moralists, cowards, and wise men. Listen and you will hear such a small explosion in this paragraph.

All this rambling may seem pointless and a waste of time, but it is not. There is absolutely no haste—I can walk the hundred-yard dash in a full day—and anyone who prefers may toss this story aside and take up something in *The Cosmopolitan*. I am not asking anyone to stand by. I am not promising golden apples to all who are patient. I am sitting in my room, living my life, tapping my typewriter. I am sitting in the presence of my father, who has been gone from the earth so many years. Every two or three minutes I look up into his melancholy face to see how he is taking it all. It is like looking into a mirror, for I see myself. I am almost as old as he was when the photograph was taken and I am wearing the very same moustache he wore at the time. I worship this man. All my life I have worshipped him. When both of us lived on the earth I was much too young to exchange so much as a single word with him, consciously, but ever since I have come to consciousness and articulation we have had many long silent conversations. I say to him, "Ah, you melancholy Armenian, you; how marvelous your life has been!" And he replies gently, "Be humble, my son. Seek God."

My father was a writer, too. He was an unpublished writer. I have all his great manuscripts, his great poems and stories, written in our native language, which I cannot read. Two or three times each year I bring out all my father's papers and stare for hours at his contribution to the literature of the world. Like myself, I am pleased to say, he was desperately poor; poverty trailed him like a hound, as the expression is. Most of his poems and stories were written on wrapping paper which he folded into small books. Only his journal is in English (which he spoke and wrote perfectly), and it is full of lamentations. In New York, according to this journal, my father had only two moods: *sad* and *very sad*. About thirty years ago he was alone in that city, and he was trying to earn enough money to pay for the passage of his wife and three children to the new world. He was a janitor. Why should I withhold this fact? There is nothing shameful about a great man's being a janitor in America. In the old country he was a man of honour, a professor, and he was called Agha, which means approximately lord. Unfortunately, he was also a revolutionist, as all good Armenians are. He wanted the handful of people of his race to be free. He wanted them to enjoy liberty, and so he was placed in jail every now and then. Finally, it got so bad that if he did not leave the old country, he would kill and be killed. He knew English, he had read Shakespeare and Swift in English, and so he came to this country. And they made a janitor of him.

After a number of years of hard work his family joined him in New York. In California, according to my father's journal, matters for a while were slightly better for him; he mentioned sunshine and magnificent bunches of grapes. So he tried farming. At first he worked for other farmers, then he made a down payment on a small farm of his own. But he was a rotten farmer. He was a man of books, a professor; he loved good clothes. He loved leisure and comfort, and like myself he hated machinery.

My father's vineyard was about eleven miles east of the nearest town, and all the farmers near by were in the habit of going to town once or twice a week on bicycles, which were the vogue at that time and a trifle faster than a horse and buggy. One hot afternoon in August a tall individual in very fine clothes was seen moving forward in long leisurely strides over a hot and dusty country road. It was my father. My people told me this story about the man, so that I might understand what a fool he was and not be like him. Someone saw my father. It was a neighbour farmer who was returning from the city on a bicycle. This man was amazed.

"Agha," he said, "where are you going?"

"To town," my father said.

"But, Agha," said the farmer, "you cannot do this thing. It is eleven miles to town and you look . . . People will laugh at you in such clothes."

"Let them laugh," my father said. "These are my clothes. They fit me."

"Yes, yes, of course they fit you," said the farmer, "but such clothes do not seem right out here, in this dust and heat. Everyone wears overalls out here, Agha."

"Nonsense," said my father. He went on walking.

The farmer followed my father, whom he now regarded as insane.

"At least, at least," he said, "if you insist on wearing those clothes, at least you will not humiliate yourself by *walking* to town. You will at least accept the use of my bicycle."

This farmer was a close friend of my father's family, and he had great respect for my father. He meant well, but my father was dumbfounded. He stared at the man with horror and disgust.

"What?" he shouted. "You ask me to mount one of those crazy contraptions? You ask me to tangle myself in that ungodly piece of junk?" (The Armenian equivalent of junk is a good deal more violent and horrible.) "Man was not made for such absurd inventions," my father said. "Man was not placed on the earth to tangle himself in junk. He was placed here to stand erect and to walk with his feet."

And away he went.

Ah, you can be sure that I worship this man. And now, alone in my room, thinking of these things, tapping out this story, I want to show you that I and my father are the same man.

I shall come soon to the matter of the typewriter, but there is no hurry. I am a story-teller, not an aviator. I am not carrying myself across the Atlantic in the cockpit of an airplane, which moves at the rate of two hundred and fifty miles per hour.

It is Monday of this year, 1933, and I am trying to gather as much of eternity into this story as possible. When next this story is read I may be with my father in the earth we both love and I may have sons alive on the surface of this, old earth, young fellows whom I shall ask to be humble, as my father has asked me to be humble.

In a moment a century may have elapsed, and I am doing what I can to keep this moment solid and alive.

Musicians have been known to weep at the loss of a musical instrument, or at its injury. To a great violinist his violin is a part of his identity. I am a young man with a dark mind, and a dark way in general, a sullen and serious way. The earth is mine, but not the world. If I am taken away from language, if I am placed in the street, as one more living entity, I become nothing, not even a shadow. I have less honour than the grocer's clerk, less dignity than the doorman at the St. Francis Hotel, less identity than the driver of a taxi-cab.

And for the past six months I have been separated from my writing, and I have been nothing, or I have been walking about unalive, some indistinct shadow in a nightmare of the universe. It is simply that without conscious articulation, without words, without language, I do not exist as myself. I have no meaning, and I might just as well be dead and nameless. It is blasphemous for any living man to live in such a manner. It is an outrage to God. It means that we have got nowhere after all these years.

It is for this reason, now that I have my typewriter again, and have beside me a bundle of clean writing paper, and am sitting in my room, full of tobacco smoke, with my father's photograph watching over me—it is for this reason that I feel I have just been resurrected from the dead. I love and worship life, living senses, functioning minds. I love consciousness. I love precision. And life is to be created by every man who has the breath of God within him; and every man is to create his own consciousness, and his own precision, for these things do not exist of themselves. Only confusion and error and ugliness exist of themselves. I have said that I am deeply religious. I am. I believe that I live, and you've got to be religious to believe so miraculous a thing. And I am grateful and I am humble. I *do* live, so let the years repeat themselves eternally, for I am sitting in my room, stating in words the truth of my being, squeezing the fact from meaninglessness and imprecision. And the living of this moment can never be effaced. It is beyond time.

I despise commerce. I am a young man with no money. There are times when a young man can use a small sum of money to very good advantage, there are times when money to him, because of what it can purchase, is the most important thing of his life, I despise commerce, but I admit that I have some respect for money. It is, after all, pretty important, and it was the lack of it, year after year, that finally killed my father. It wasn't right for a man so poor to wear the sort of clothes he knew he deserved; so my father died. I would like to have enough money to enable me to live simply and to write my life. Years ago, when I laboured in behalf of industry and progress and so on, I purchased a small portable typewriter, brand new, for sixty-five dollars. (And what an enormous lot of money that is, if you are poor.) At first this machine was strange to me and I was annoyed by the racket it made when it was in use; late at night this racket was unbearably distressing. It resembled more than anything else silence which has been magnified a thousand times, if such a thing can be. But after a year or two I began to feel a genuine attachment toward the machine, and loved it as a good pianist, who respects music, loves his piano. I never troubled to clean the machine and no matter how persistently I pounded upon it, the machine did not weaken and fall to pieces. I had great respect for it.

And then, in a fit of despondency, I placed this small machine in its case and carried it to the city. I left it in the establishment of a money-lender, and walked through the city with fifteen dollars in my pocket. I was sick of being poor.

I went first to a bootblack and had my shoes polished. When a bootblack is shining my shoes I place him in my place in the chair and I descend and polish his shoes. It is an experience in humility.

Then I went to a theatre. I sat among people to see myself in patterns of Hollywood. I sat and dreamed, looking into the faces of beautiful women. Then I went to a restaurant and sat at a table and ordered all the different kinds of food I ever thought I would like to eat. I ate two dollars' worth of food. The waiter thought I was out of my head, but I told him everything was going along first rate. I tipped the waiter. Then I went out into the city again and began walking along the dark streets, the streets where the women are. I was tired of being poor. I put my typewriter in hock and I began to spend the money. No one, not even the greatest writer, can go on being poor hour after hour, year after year. There is such a thing as saying to hell with art. That's what I said.

After a week I became a little more sober. After a month I got to be very sober and I began to want my typewriter again. I began to want to put words on paper again. To make another beginning. To say something and see if it was the right thing. But I had no money. Day after day I had this longing for my typewriter.

This is the whole story. I don't suppose this is a very artful ending, but it is the ending just the same. The point is this: *day after day I longed for my typewriter*.

This morning I got it back. It is before me now and I am tapping at it, and this is what I have written.

5

The Select Bookshop of
Mr Rao and Mr Murthy

When I first saw Bangalore, in the spring of 1960, it was a town of wide streets, bungalows, gardens, parks and small waterbodies. From the airport to the city the roads were lined with flowering laburnum trees. There wasn't much traffic in those days and I explored most of the town on foot. Among other places, I discovered the Sampingi tank, where small boys dived into the water off the backs of their buffaloes. The tank, boys and buffaloes are long gone; I think a car park occupies the site now.

Strolling along M.G. Road I discovered an 'old curiosity shop' full of books, pictures, collections of postcards, curios, relics of colonial times. I stopped to browse and picked up a number of old books, magazines and postcards, which I brought back with me to New Delhi, where I was living and working at the time.

The shop was run by Mr K.B.K. Rao, and over the years, I stayed in touch with him and, after his demise, with his son, Mr K.K.S. Murthy, who would send me handwritten lists of books that he thought would interest me. And so I augmented my small library with a number of titles of an off-beat nature, not easily found elsewhere.

The shop was called the Select Bookshop, and it has since moved to Brigade Road. I met Mr Murthy in the early 1990s, when I was in Bangalore again, writing a history of the Bangalore Golf Club, the one on High Grounds. This too has become something of a rare book!

Mr Murthy continues to send me his handwritten lists, and the books keep piling up. Due to shortage of space, I give away some of them. But there are many that I like reading twice, or dipping into from time to time, and these I cling to, much to the annoyance of Rakesh's wife, Beena, who needs more space for furniture, cushions and crockery. So books infiltrate into the dining-room, and cups and saucers turn up on my bookshelves. How is she to feed me if there is nowhere to set down a cucumber, a bag of atta, or a bundle of onions and potatoes! In the end we co-exist quite happily, since I do need her potato crisps as much as I need my *Pickwick Papers*.

So let me find a fascinating book to share with you, something that came to me from Mr Murthy's bookshop.

Or better still, let's see what's in the latest parcel that he has sent me. My reading tastes being fairly varied, I ordered a mixed bunch of books quite at random, for I love discovering the unusual, the little-known, the forgotten, and even the eccentric. Sometimes a little gem turns up; or a neglected masterpiece. Sometimes they are really ordinary, justifiably forgotten, and soon discarded. But more often than not there is something worth keeping.

Like this 'Tale of a Child', tucked away in an old volume of *The World's Greatest Short Stories*.

It purports to have been written by a child, and in every respect it is childlike, but its Hungarian author was a Doctor of Literature who wrote, not only in his own language but also in French and English. This lovely story was written in English, and it captures the innocence and curiosity of a small boy as he comes to terms with the adult world. I found it quite moving. It has humour and pathos and the bloom of childhood. How I wish I'd written it!

'The Tale of a Child' (1932)
by Josef Bard

. . . To-day it is very warm and we shall go and bathe in the Danube. We are not allowed to bathe in the Danube because it is dangerous but we know a spot where there is a bad smell because it is near a factory where they make leather from the hide of oxen. There the water is shallow and we can all stand up in the water. Jacob too can stand up though he is small but he is very wise and Andreas can swim and we all cling to the neck of Roka my dog. Jacob holds most of Roka's neck although Roka is my dog but Jacob is very frightened of the Danube and he would be punished if he drowned, because his father told him so. His father is a man with a curly long black beard and apart from that he is also our grocer and he has black rings under his eyes. I don't like Jacob's father because he always pats me on the head and then my hair smells of cheese, and I must wash always although I have washed already. But I like Jacob because he is wise. I don't know how but he is very wise. We all play at marbles after class and we all lose. But Jacob never plays because his father told him so. But he exchanges our bad marbles for better marbles and we buy them from him. Andreas says this is because Jacob is a Jew and his father told him so. I like Andreas but I think he is a liar. He told me the other day there is a dead mason hidden in the walls of every big house. The mason was alive when they walled him in but now he is dead. I don't believe it but I don't like it. Andreas' father is a gentleman who builds houses for others and he told him so.

I am sure Andreas is a liar. Now when we have all come out of the water and were drying ourselves in the grass so that nobody could tell we had been in the Danube and Roka sat down on our clothes and made them wet and we drove Roka away with stones although we all held his neck in the water, now Andreas was chewing a leaf of grass and told us he saw God yesterday early in the afternoon.

"You are a liar," I said to Andreas. Jacob said nothing but he smiled. He is very wise when he smiles. I saw that Jacob also thought that Andreas was a little liar.

"I am not a liar. I came down to the river and I saw a big white cloud in the sky just like a feather-pillow and God flew out, dipped his feet in the water, smiled at me and flew back again."

So we looked up into the sky. We saw white clouds, fluffy like the sheep in the village and not a bit like feather-pillows. I knew Andreas was a liar. And God simply couldn't fly out of such a cloud.

Still I was envious. I shall be ten years old after two years and I haven't seen God yet. I thought maybe Jacob had more luck. So I asked him: "Jacob, have you see God?" But Jacob looked frightened and he said he must not speak of God because his father told him so. Then I turned to Andreas again and said to him: "Andreas, I know you are just lying. Look in my eyes and say again that you saw God!" And Andreas who was lying on his back turned round on his belly and looked at me. Andreas is very beautiful. He has long flaxen locks and his face is very white and his eyes are like brown fruit-drops when you have sucked them and taken them out of your mouth and then hold them in your hand to see how much is left. But I could not look into his eyes as mother looks into mine. His eyes were not in his face they were just like clouds in the sky. So I just said: "Andreas, I believe you are a liar." Still I am not quite sure. And then we all went home, Jacob and Andreas and Roka and I and we never said another word.

. . . to-day Father eats the marrow-bone. When Father is away I eat the marrow-bone, when he is at home he gives me a bit of the marrow, on a bit of bread, salted and peppered. I was waiting for my bit to-day but he forgot me. He often is like that. I said: "Father—" because I am told to call him Father and not Daddie—"Father, Andreas told me he saw God in the afternoon—do you think it is true?" But Father finished the marrow-bone and said I was a donkey. I looked sad and then Mother told Father "don't be rude to the child." Then Father said that Mother spoils me. Then they quarrelled. Then I stopped sulking. I love Mother. All the boys love their Mothers but they respect their Fathers. But my Mother is very beautiful. She has long hair and big eyes and a big mouth and she is soft and plump.

So we were all eating quietly in the garden under the mulberry-tree and the ripe mulberries kept dropping from the tree into my rice-pudding, so wonderful is nature. But still I wanted to know whether Andreas saw God. When Father left the table I asked Mother: "Mother dear—do you think Andreas really saw God?" But she looked tired because Father had not kissed her when he left the table because they quarrelled and she sighed. She said: "The questions you ask! How should I know?" And then she also left the table and followed Father into the house.

Mother is very beautiful and plump but she never answers my questions. I shall ask Kate, our cook who is plumper than Mother but not so very beautiful. She has already told me where babies come from. She will know whether Andreas, the little liar, saw God or not.

. . . to-day I have not spoken to Andreas in school because I am not sure whether he is a liar or not. This is a warm morning. The sun is shining and we all wanted to laugh but we had no chance because our teacher Prunk spoke only of serious things and had the birch in his hand. Jacob brought some old stamps and we are all collecting stamps because Jacob says it is the best way to learn the map of the world. Slezak sits behind me and he is the son of our washer-woman, but he hates Jacob. But Slezak is very stupid and our teacher Prunk told him so. We are all a little afraid of Slezak because he is very strong and hits us on the jaw. He says the English all hit each other on the jaw which makes them very strong. Jacob has many English stamps because he has an uncle there who sends them to him. His uncle hits nobody on the jaw but publishes books which others have written, and his father told him so. But when Slezak hit Jacob on the jaw, Jacob smiled mildly and asked him "is this what you have learned from your Reverend Father and Jesus Christ?" And Slezak said Jacob crucified Jesus Christ and now he must be hit on the jaw. And we were all very excited and Prunk came in and birched Slezak and told the class we were all Hungarians and we must love each other because anyhow we are only few and our enemies are many. Then he read us a poem which said that the earth is the hat of God and Hungary is a bunch of flowers on the top of the hat. This was written by a great poet called Petöfi, who fell in the battle when the Hungarians were just conquering the Russians. We Hungarians have the habit of winning all the battles but this we lost because we were already tired by conquering the Austrians. The Russians and the Austrians are our enemies and so are others we haven't yet learned about and Prunk says our enemies are many and our friends are few and we must prepare to be proud when the moment arrives when we shall die for Hungary. But we still have time and so we must learn Petöfi's poem by heart and we must not forget that now the Austrians are our friends and our King Francis Joseph rules over them too but he loves only the Hungarians and he only rules over the Austrians because his father told him to. Our King is hanging on the wall and he is very dignified and hairy, and he is now very old but he was young when he began to be a King. When we sing the National Anthem we all look at him and he looks back at us very dignified and hairy.

We all read aloud what is called the poem and it was difficult to remember it because the lines all end the same way, but we were all very proud that we were so few and always conquered our enemies who were many and Slezak wanted to go to the lavatory, which he always wants to do when we must learn something by heart. And Jacob stood up and asked our teacher how could the earth be the hat of God when he told us that the earth was round like a rubber-ball. Jacob is very wise and when we were reading the poem we had quite forgotten that Prunk told us the earth was round. We all looked at Prunk and we all saw clearly he could say just nothing. But he was trying very hard. He said Petőfi was a very great poet and very great poets are permitted to say sometimes what is not quite true. But we all thought that Jacob conquered Prunk. But perhaps Prunk told the truth. And perhaps Andreas is not a little liar but only a great poet?

. . . to-day Grandma arrived from town. Grandma is a much older lady than Mother but this is only natural. She is small and she always smoothes her mouth with her fingers because her teeth are not natural. But she was sad to-day because my Uncle Berti came with her who is also her son and Uncle Berti is ill. I don't know what is wrong with Uncle Berti they only say he is mad. I like Uncle Berti because he is so funny, and he sometimes pushes his spoon under his chin because he can't find his mouth and pours the soup under his collar which is a good joke from a grown-up man but Grandma looks sad and kicks me under the table when I laugh. Uncle Berti worked in town and he was almost a bank-director but not quite but this was before he poured the soup under his collar. Now he lives with Grandma who is also his Mother. And he is very big and very silent but he likes to play with me when I play in the garden building castles from mudpies. And Mother and Grandma sat under the mulberry tree and watched us and we sat on the ground and when I turned round I think Mother and Grandma were blowing their noses and I think they wept although Uncle Berti made much better mudpies than I did. And then they went into the house and I followed them to wash my hands and I heard them talk although I did not want to listen but they had not seen me. And Mother was afraid Uncle Berti would get wild one day and wanted him to go to a place where he could get wild safely. But Grandma only wept and cursed Uncle Berti's wife but he had two wives and this was unhealthy for him especially when they both loved him. And then I went to the kitchen and just heard Kate the cook say to the maid that Uncle Berti had water in his head but when they saw me they said no more.

And so I went back to Uncle Berti and he was all right doing well with mudpies. And I sat down next to Uncle Berti and looked in his eyes and they were blue but they were not there. And I thought he might perhaps know whether Andreas saw God, so I asked him. And he only said: "Very-berry-mulberry" and then he smiled. And then he stood up and was very tall and his hair I saw was white and he said "let us go to Church I would like to pray." So I took him by the hand and we went into the house and I said to Mother "Uncle Berti and I want to go to Church." And Mother looked frightened but Grandma said it was all right. And so we walked out, I holding his hand and I took him to the chapel although it was three o'clock in the afternoon and God is seldom at home at that hour. And it was very dark and cool in the chapel and candles burnt in the corners and I was not comfortable because Uncle Berti held my hand very tight. And I don't go to Church because Father says he hates all the priests and if there is God there is only one who also hates the priests. But it is beautiful in our chapel it smells good not like near the river where they make leather from the hide of oxen. And the lady-saints were very beautiful and they all had flowers on the altar. We just stood in the middle of the chapel and we were quite alone and it was very silent. And Uncle Berti whispered into my ear whether I could see a gentleman-saint because he would like to pray before a gentleman-saint and not before a lady-saint to-day. And I found him one in the right corner who was tied to a tree and he was very naked but there were arrows in him. And Uncle Berti let my hand go and fell on his knees and began to pray, but it seemed to have little sense and I wondered whether the saint would understand what he was saying. Then Uncle Berti wept and he wept very loud and I was afraid because it was very silent and we were alone and I had heard Mother say Uncle Berti might get wild. But it was not true because he stood up and was very quiet and stroked my hand and thanked me for taking him to the chapel. It was all right what he said, so I told him why did he let himself be called mad. Then he laughed and he laughed just as loud as he wept before, and I got frightened again. But he became quiet again and we walked out of the chapel and he said he wanted to buy me something. So I took him to Jacob's father who is the grocer and I chose a box of green lizards made of rubber-candy. And Jacob's father made big eyes and forgot to pat me on the head which made me grateful. And Uncle Berti shook hands with Jacob's father and forgot to pay and we all went back to Mother and Grandma.

Then Grandma and Uncle Berti went to the station and we accompanied them and Uncle Berti was so big and Grandma very small but she led him by the hand. And Uncle Berti was very pale and when he shook hands with me, my heart hurt because I was now sorry for him. I wished he had something better than water in his head.

. . . to-day we went to swim in the Danube again where it stinks but it is safe and I kept my head out of water because I was afraid water might get into my head through my ears as with Uncle Berti. We are friends again with Andreas and I always like Jacob because he is wise. And we went rather late and we rolled about naked and Jacob was different because he was taken into the bosom of Abraham that way and it happened when he was eight days old and his father told him so. Jacob has very thin legs and thin arms and Andreas is much more beautiful but Andreas rolled very close to me and I told him I didn't like it because we must only love girls and Kate the cook told me so. And so Andreas rolled on his belly and his bottom was turned towards me and it seemed beautiful but it was his bottom and bottoms are ugly because my Mother told me so and you must never show it except when you are alone and the doctor asks you to. I told this to Andreas but he laughed and then he lied again because he must always lie except when he is a great poet. Andreas lied that children are made of marble and rose-leaves and they are beautiful everywhere and we only cover our bottoms because otherwise we would be too beautiful for our parents. So I called him a liar because I know babies are made by mothers and Slezak the son of our washer-woman brought me the cord which came out with him into the world and he found it in a drawer and it was wrapped in a paper and it was brown and horrid.

And Jacob said we must not bother about this, but collect stamps in peace and learn the map of the world because his father told him so.

But I still called Andreas a liar because I saw our dog Roka starting to make babies to his wife and Kate, the cook told me Father was not different. Andreas did not answer but smelt the daisies in the grass. Then he said he didn't care what we knew but he dreamt babies were made of marbles and rose-leaves. Now I knew he was lying again because I dreamt that Uncle Berti came back and I broke a hole in his head with my hatchet and all the water flowed out and our teacher Prunk was drowned in the flood but it was not true because in the morning I saw that Prunk was still alive and teaching history. I wanted Jacob to be on my side against Andreas but Jacob is very wise and he only wants to collect stamps in peace.

So I teased Andreas who was still smelling the daisies which I know have no smell and told him if he knew everything did he know what the stars were. Andreas said he knew but he couldn't say it because he didn't know the words. So I asked him did he know what the moon was. And Andreas said the moon is a pale woman who is looking for a lost world. And then I got frightened just like in the chapel when Uncle Berti wept aloud and I thought perhaps water had got into the ears of Andreas because I also see ghosts in the dark but I know they are not there because my Mother told me so. So I asked him what the sun is and Andreas lifted his head and said the sun is an angry flame which wants to burn everything and the earth is running away from him because he is frightened. And Jacob and I were also frightened and it was now dark and Jacob said we must not ask more questions from Andreas because he is perhaps a prophet and we must be happy when prophets are silent because his father told him so. And we all walked home and said no more.

. . . to-day I saw Kate the cook drinking rum in the kitchen but I shall not tell Mother because Kate is my friend and always answers my questions and Mother is more beautiful but she never answers my questions and Father is always angry. And Kate gave some rum to Peti the milkman who always smells of what the cows leave when they don't behave properly and who is waiting on the cows. And Peti the milkman started to be like Roka my dog when he joined his wife but Kate pushed him back and asked him whether he was not ashamed before the child which was me. And then I remembered that Lola had her birthday and she had asked me to come and have some of her birthday cake and I had not asked Mother because now it was after dinner and I had to go to bed. So I asked Kate to let me in through the kitchen door when I came back and then I went into the garden and picked white and red roses which she liked and walked to Lola's house because I think I love Lola and I would like to marry Lola if she could preserve herself till I grow up. Because Lola is already very big and her hair is perfumed when she kisses me and she lives in a big house, with a big orchard where a brook flows through and she has many young men playing the piano with her which is very musical. And when I arrived she was playing but she stopped and kissed me again and her hair was again perfumed. And there were many people and they were eating sandwiches and Lola wore a long white dress and her arms were puffed but this was only her dress and not her arms. And everybody was very nice to me though they laughed and a fat man who played with Lola pinched my cheeks, and I told him I didn't like that and I thought he was stupid. I said this because I saw him breathe down on Lola's neck when she played the piano and I love Lola. And Lola saw that I was angry and she said we two will go out into the garden, and so we went out and we sat down under a cherry tree and we sat on the grass and I put my head on Lola's white neck and kissed it which Lola said I must not do. And Lola was sad and she looked up at the moon and she sighed. And she said "do you see the moon?" And I said "yes, I see the moon she is like a pale woman looking for a lost world." And then I blushed because I remembered that I had heard this from Andreas, that little liar. But Lola did not remember it and she kissed me on the mouth and said that it was very beautiful and asked me whether I could say something else as beautiful. Then I said the sun is an angry flame which wants to burn everything and the earth is running away from him because he is frightened. Then I blushed again because I remembered that I heard this also from Andreas the little liar. But Lola kissed me on the mouth again and she said how poetic children are and I saw she thought of the fat man who was not so poetic and then she said I must come when I had something beautiful to say and that she would always kiss me. So we parted in the garden and I did not go back to the house with her because I didn't like the fat man but Lola went back and I walked to my home. I was very happy and wondered what the stars were but then Father was waiting for me in the kitchen and he said he would break my bones if I left the house without permission at night and he began doing so, but Mother came and told him not to be rude to the child and then they quarrelled and I hurried to my room before they had finished and I thought I hated to be beaten and I would kill whoever dares to beat me, only fathers unfortunately can't be killed because my Mother told me so. So I went to bed and I dreamt of Lola but it was not true because I could not remember it in the morning.

. . . to-day Slezak was late for school because he said his mother had borne him a brother which is curious because Slezak has no father. But we did not ask questions because Prunk told us more about our History and he said we Hungarians were somewhere else a thousand years ago and we had the habit of multiplying ourselves quickly so we went out to find another home so we came to Hungary which is where we now are and we conquered the people we found here because we had the habit of winning all the battles. But it was not easy to find Hungary because it was far from the place where we multiplied ourselves, but our very own Battle-god sent us a bird and he flew ahead of us and when we arrived he flew back to our very own Battle-god and so Prunk said we have been in Hungary now for over a thousand years and had much glory and we have fought against the Turks who also belonged to our enemies but we haven't yet learnt about them and we have suffered much glory because we were only few and our enemies were many. And we were all very proud but then Jacob stood up and asked Prunk why we had so many enemies. Prunk knows much and has a big wart on his forehead but Jacob is wise and Prunk thought a little while and then said we are the bunch of flowers on God's hat and our neighbours are all envious of us. Then we all stood up and sang the National Anthem and our King Francis Joseph hanging on the wall listened to us and he listened to our promise that we would all die here because we couldn't go elsewhere. Then Prunk left us for half an hour to give us time to wash our hands and eat our bread and butter and we all stood round Slezak who was sad because now his mother can't wash for a month and he did not want a brother because they are very poor and his father died when they hit him on the head with a bottle of rum. Slezak said it was Peti the milkman who did it to his mother but he would buy a gun and shoot him. Then Andreas pulled me by the sleeve and we all left Slezak and whispered because Andreas asked us to collect money for Slezak because he is very poor. And we all promised to give him our pocket money for the week and to ask our parents to give him money. Then Slezak had to go to Prunk's room and he came back weeping because Prunk asked him to leave the school. And we all hated Prunk and called him an ugly wart which he had on his forehead. And when Prunk came back to teach history we all stood up and Jacob walked in front of us and asked Prunk in the name of the class to take back Slezak because Slezak is innocent because he did not tell Peti the milkman to do it to his mother. Then Prunk was very angry and told

Jacob to go back to his place and said we should not know about such things and that Slezak was a bad influence. Then he taught us more about our glorious past and how we conquered our enemies and how our Kings helped us but I don't remember because we did not listen because we thought of Slezak. And when the class was over Prunk saw that we were all sad and he said he would talk about Slezak to the headmaster. Then we all cheered and were proud again of our glorious past.

. . . to-day is Friday evening and I was permitted to go to Jacob's house and have dinner with them because I gave some old stamps to Jacob and he was grateful. And it was very warm in the room and we all kept our hats on our heads because Jacob's God likes that and also we were more than thirteen because otherwise Jacob's God is not present. And Jacob's father was very clean and he had a white stole on his neck and he prayed loud and we all murmured and then we had soup with big dumplings in it and we had roast goose with much stuffings. And Jacob's relatives were there and they had beards but the women were only fat. Jacob has no mother but his aunt cooks for him and she is called Hannah and she is only half-witted but she cooks well. Jacob says Jews are wise, but when they are not they are very stupid. It was very hot and we were not happy because Jacob's God really lives in Palestine and only comes for a short visit to our village. And I said to Jacob now we will go to my garden and eat fruit from the trees.

And then we walked home which is not far because our village is small. And Jacob was sad because he had no mother and Friday night he always remembers her. So I told him stories to amuse him how the Austrian villagers carry ladders sideways through the forest and cut down the trees to make way. But Jacob was still sad and I looked up at the stars and wondered what they were and whether Andreas the little liar had found the words for them. Then I told Jacob about Lola and that I was going to marry her if she can preserve herself until I grow up but Jacob only smiled and he said I would forget her when I grew up. I know Jacob is very wise but I don't believe what he said. But when we turned into my garden we could not eat fruit because we found Kate the cook weeping under the mulberry tree and Father came out and told her she must go away, because she wanted to push the carving knife into Peti the milkman because Peti did it to Slezak's mother and he also did it to Kate, and Peti also had a wife. Peti must be very healthy because now he has three wives and has no water in his head and Uncle Berti had only two wives and his head was full of water. But Mother came out and she is very kind and she patted Kate on the cheek and told her to stay and she sent Father back into the house. And then a policeman came because Kate had just scratched Peti with the carving knife and the policeman wanted Kate to go with him but Father said everything was all right and gave a cigar to the policeman and then Peti came with his head bandaged and said it was all a misunderstanding and Kate remained with us but we shall get milk elsewhere. And Father said to Peti that he would break his bones if he ever dared to come to our house again but Mother said don't be rude to the poor fellow and sent Father into the house. Then Kate went to bed weeping and Peti and the policeman left and I took Jacob to the garden gate because it was now late. And Jacob who is so wise said to me it is much better to collect stamps in peace. He said love is very unhappy always because his father told him so.

. . . to-day when Father was eating my marrow-bone I asked him to give me money because we are collecting for Slezak in school. But Father said he had no money to throw away and I looked sad and Mother said to Father don't be rude to the child. And then they quarrelled. And when we were left alone under the mulberry-tree Mother said she would give me money but I must be nicer to Father. And I said I am very nice to him but he never talks to me. Mother said Father works for us and he is tired and we must cheer him up. All fathers must be cheered up. They all work for their wives and children and when they don't they are not happy. So I must not forget to greet Father when I see him in the morning which I always do. So I asked Mother why she married Father and she said the questions children ask and left me alone. Mother is plump and beautiful but I don't understand her. I understand Kate much better who is now very plump. But I love Mother and she gave me money for Slezak. Slezak is now back in school with us and he wanted to give me his cord which is in a tissue paper because he is grateful because I collected for him but I did not want his cord because it is horrid. Slezak is very stupid and he hit Jacob on the jaw because he said it will make him strong because the English all hit each other on the jaw which makes them strong. But Jacob always says he hates violence because his father told him so.

Slezak is also very happy because the brother his mother bore him recently died yesterday and now Slezak is again his mother's only orphan. And he asked us to come and see him because he is now in a coffin over the washing-tub and candles burn. And in the afternoon we all went to see Slezak's brother, Jacob and Andreas and Roka and I but Roka had to wait outside in the courtyard. And Slezak's brother was in a small white coffin and Slezak's mother who is our washer-woman when she has no babies gave

rum to her friends who came to see her and she wanted
to give rum to us too but we did not want it. So we just
stared at the candles and we were silent and Jacob was sad
because he remembered his mother as on Friday evenings
and Andreas was very pale and he whispered something
but I could not hear it. Then we all coughed because we
wanted to go out and Slezak's mother thanked us for
coming and thanked us for collecting money for Slezak
who is only a silly bully. Then she wept and her cheeks
were all very red like apples and when she wiped her tears
I saw her hands were all red from washing. So we coughed
again and blew our noses and went out into the courtyard
because the room opens on a courtyard which is not clean.
And Roka was chewing an old bone which he had found
on the dustheap and we took it away from him. But Slezak
only stood there leaning against the door and he looked on
the ground and he forgot to hit Jacob on the jaw to make
him strong which he always does.

. . . to-day we are very excited because Aunt Leonie
arrived who is also my Mother's sister. And she married
an Austrian who lives in Vienna where also lives our King
Francis Joseph when he rules over the Austrians. But Aunt
Leonie married long ago and now she has children and
she brought one called Pamperl which sounds silly but

is Austrian because the Viennese are also Austrian. Aunt Leonie married Uncle Pepi because he was beautiful and he sang songs about Vienna which is also beautiful and he was very funny and because she thought Uncle Pepi was almost a bank-director but he was only a great traveller for business and he always was travelling when Aunt Leonie had the babies. So we all sat under the mulberry-tree and Aunt Leonie wept and she had anyhow watery eyes and Father said why did she marry Uncle Pepi and she must go back to Uncle Pepi because now they had four children and then Aunt Leonie finished her cake and wept some more and Mother said to Father don't be rude to my sister and then we were left alone.

Then Mother asked Aunt Leonie what she intended to do and Aunt Leonie said the children should go for a walk. And I took Pamperl by the hand which is very soft and we walked out and Pamperl who has a sallow face and a lace collar talked to me but it was Austrian or Viennese and it sounded funny but I could not understand it. So we walked to the river and I led Pamperl through the dam where the water is very wild and I thought it was a pity the Austrians were our friends now and our King Francis Joseph rules over them also, because otherwise I would push Pamperl into the water and then Uncle Pepi and Aunt Leonie would have only three children and we would all be happier. But

I hurried through the dam and I took Pamperl to where we bathe and I wanted Pamperl to bathe in the river because I thought Pamperl might drown without my help and then we should have one enemy less when the Austrians will be our enemies again, because we are only few and our enemies are many. But Pamperl shrieked and so I walked back with him to our house. And there we found Uncle Pepi who is very bald but has a lovely beard and a moustache like our King Francis Joseph but he is not so dignified because he always laughs. And Uncle Pepi followed my Aunt from Vienna because he thought now that he loved her better than Gullash and beer which he loves very much. And he took Pamperl on his knees and gave him beer and he sang a song about a Viennese cab which all Viennese sing and is also loved by our King Francis Joseph when he rules over the Austrians. Mother was sad and told Aunt Leonie that she must go back to Vienna tomorrow. And we went to bed but I slept only little because Uncle Pepi sang about the Viennese cab all night long.

. . . to-day Slezak hit the butcher's son on the jaw who called him a bastard and then Slezak hit him again and Jacob asked Slezak whether he had learnt this from his Reverend Father and Jesus Christ our Saviour because Jacob hates violence and wants us all to collect stamps in peace.

Slezak hit Jacob on the jaw but only to make him strong. But I stood up for Slezak because he was called a bastard which was true but not very beautiful. And Slezak wanted to give me his cord again but I did not want it because it is horrid. Then he wanted to give me holy pictures which he got from our Reverend Father because Slezak has very good marks in religion and the Reverend Father calls him a lost sheep who is now back with the flock. And the holy picture was very beautiful and the Virgin Mary on it looked like Lola whom I love only Lola has no baby. But I did not take the holy picture because if there is a God there is only one who hates the priests because my Father told me so. Then Slezak who is very grateful because I have also collected money for him said he would tell me a secret but I must swear not to tell it to anybody else. And he told me there is a house in our village which stands alone in a meadow and which is always shut with green shutters during the day because the ladies who live there always sleep during the day and only wake up at night. And they are all very beautiful because they are all painted and perfumed and he knows one lady called Amanta who looks like the Virgin Mary on the picture only she is not a virgin although she has no baby. And they have many visitors during the night but they are all men who want no babies. And I thought Slezak was lying to me and I told him so but Slezak swore it was all true because his mother is washing for the ladies who sleep during the day and it is all very beautiful and full of mirrors and he went one day with his mother to help with the laundry and his mother told him not to look but he looked very much. And now I remembered I had seen the house with the green shutters alone in the meadow but I did not know ladies lived there who were sleeping during the day just like in the fairy-tales. So when I went home from school I asked Mother to come with me for a walk and she was happy because I always go with Jacob and Andreas. And then I wanted to go where the house with the green shutters stood and we saw it standing alone in the meadow. I told Mother to look what a beautiful house it was. But she blushed and said it was an ugly house and I must never go near it. And I said I thought it was the house of the Sleeping Beauty which I read in the tales. But Mother said this was a very bad house and I must promise never to go near it. Mother is plump and very beautiful but she never answers my questions. Kate the cook always answers them. So I went to the kitchen to ask Kate about the fairy castle which stands alone in the meadow because I also dreamt of the fairies but I can't remember. But Peti the milkman was there although my Father will break his bones because he told him so. Peti still smells of cows but Kate our cook loves him again. He also gave me a whistle which he brought for me but I will wash it because Peti made it wet with his mouth. And Kate is now very plump and she weeps but she says she loves Peti again because the baby died which Peti did to Slezak's mother and Peti's wife has also the dry rot and she will die soon and then Peti will marry Kate. And we were all very happy and Kate gave him goose-liver. And I wanted to ask Kate about the house but I thought she would not know because she is only a cook and she cooks well but she never told me a good fairy-tale. I think I shall not ask anyone about the house standing alone in the meadow because all the people I know sleep during the night and they would know nothing about the ladies who sleep during the day.

. . . to-day it is almost summer and now we know already how to add up and subtract and multiply and divide and we have learnt about most of our enemies and of our glorious past and how the Austrians have always swindled us after we have so often conquered them. And we have learned many poems and I think Petőfi wrote better poems than the one about God's hat and I have learned some and I have won a prize for reading poetry. And now we sing the anthem in tune to our King who hangs on the wall. And soon school will be over and then Mother and I shall go to the Lake Balaton which is the most beautiful lake in the world where all the Hungarians go and the Jewish Hungarians live on one end and the Roman Catholic Hungarians on the other and scattered in between are the rest. But I am not very happy because Lola whom I love will marry the fat man whom I hate and she will kiss the fat man with the same mouth with which she kissed me and she will not wait for me and preserve herself. And I am sad because Grandma came and told us that Uncle Berti is now very wild and he wants to eat his collar-buttons with his breakfast and he will die because now he has more water in his head. So I went out with Roka and looked for Jacob and then we went to find Andreas to ask him to bathe with us in the Danube. Andreas lives in a big house called a villa and he sat in the garden with his mother who has very soft hands which I like. So we kissed her hands and Roka misbehaved on the flowers and we asked Andreas to come with us. And Andreas was reading a book of poems by a poet called Shelley who was also loved by our poet Petöfi. Andreas got the book to-day because he only wants to read poetry and he said Shelley died very young and he was English but very frail, but that was perhaps because they did not hit him on the jaw to make him strong. And the father of Andreas came out into the garden and smiled at us because he is very kind and he builds houses for others and when you do that you can build some for yourself. So we all went to the Danube where it smells but it is safe and we went into the water holding Roka's neck. And I said the Danube was very beautiful this afternoon because the water was blue and green and when the leather did not stink the acacia-trees smelt sweet on the banks. But Andreas says the Danube is not very beautiful and the people who live along the Danube are all very unhappy. Andreas has travelled much already because his father takes him along with him and he has seen high mountains and he told us stories of beautiful lakes in Italy. So I was sad that the Danube was not very beautiful and we scampered back to the riverside to dry in the grass and I told Andreas to move away because we must love only girls because Kate the cook told me so. And Jacob was also very sad because his father has a bad heart and that is why he has rings under his eyes and I thought of Lola who was not faithful to me. And we all ate grass and lay on our bellies and I said when we grow up we shall also have rings under our eyes and bad hearts and perhaps water in our heads like Uncle Berti and how nice it would be to preserve ourselves. And Andreas rolled on his back and looked into the clouds which were swimming over the sky and he said everything passes away only the clouds pass and stay and I thought this was very beautiful and I could easily have told it to Lola and she would have kissed me on the mouth but now she has married the fat man who is not so poetic as we are. And I also thought this Danube river comes from Vienna where Uncle Pepi and Pamperl live and where our King Francis Joseph enjoys to hear the song of Uncle Pepi. But I got tired of thinking and I played with Roka who rolled on his back and watched Andreas who always looks into the clouds when he finds some in the sky, and I asked Andreas whether he had seen God fly out again because perhaps he said the truth after all and Andreas said he wanted to fly with the wind and hold the whole world against his heart. And he said he hated to think that one day he must die and he said there were many Gods and most of them hated us and that is why we must die. But Jacob who is very wise said that he must not say such things and there is only one God who punishes those who call him names and we must all collect stamps in peace and learn the map of the world, because his father told him so. But Andreas was not listening to him because he still watched the clouds swimming in the blue sky and I pinched him to wake him up and then he rose and we all walked home very silent and said no more.

6

The Dying Bookshop

Dehradun always had one or two small bookshops, but back in 1951, when I was sixteen and just out of school, my pocket money was barely five or ten rupees a month; and while this was sufficient to enable me to go to the cinema once or twice a week, and buy the odd magazine, it did not cover book-buying. Even those wartime Crime Club paperbacks cost two or three rupees, though a tattered Edgar Wallace or Peter Cheyney could be picked up for eight annas in the Kabari bazaar.

But there was Ideal Book Depot, a gloomy old bookshop just off Rajpur Road, where occasionally I bought a copy of *Picturegoer* or *Strand*. The owner had stopped ordering new books as there had been a sharp decline in the readership of English-language books, most of the British and Anglo-Indian families having left the country—and it would be sometime before the English-educated Indian middle-class would grow into sufficiently large numbers to comprise a book-buying public. And so the owner of Ideal Book Depot had converted his stock into a lending library, and for two rupees a month

I could borrow a book every day and exchange it the following day.

The owner of the shop was a heavy, taciturn man, who seldom left the chair behind his capacious desk, which was littered with correspondence and papers which hadn't been touched for weeks, months. He reminded me a bit of Sydney Greenstreet, the fat, jowly villain of *The Maltese Falcon* and *Casablanca*. But he was no villain, just a sad old man presiding over the decline of his book business. Five years later, when I returned from my sojourn in England, the bookshop was gone, replaced by a bicycle shop, which, in the course of time, became a provisions store.

But in 1951 Ideal Book Depot provided me with the popular literature of the period—lots of Wodehouse, Agatha Christie, 'Sapper', Dornford Yates, Ellery Queen, Rex Stout, Daphne du Maurier, James Hilton, A.J. Cronin . . .

The novels of du Maurier, Hilton and Cronin had all been filmed very successfully. Du Maurier's *Rebecca* had become one of Hitchcock's classics. James Hilton's *Lost Horizon* and *Goodbye, Mr. Chips* had been made into award-winning films. Cronin's *The Green Years*, *The Stars Look Down* and *The Keys of the Kingdom* had been turned into memorable films as well.

Many of Maugham's novels and stories had been filmed too. Who can forget Bette Davis's performance in *The Letter* and *Of Human Bondage*?

This was an era in which most of the outstanding films that came out of Hollywood or Britain were based on famous novels. I went out of my way to read the book and see the film; sometimes vice versa. The novels of Dickens made great films—*David Copperfield*, *Oliver Twist*, *Great Expectations*.

The only book I couldn't read (although I tried) was *Gone with the Wind*. I did not fare better with the film either, walking out halfway through its meandering three hours of soap-opera dialogue. There was something phoney about the book and the film—a sentimental approach to the gentry of the deep South, while glossing over the evils of slavery.

I was not averse to American writing. I enjoyed the detective novels of Ellery Queen and Rex Stout—especially the latter, whose detective Nero Wolfe never left his orchid room and his easy chair—and I have read practically everything by Jack London and Bret Harte, superb storytellers of the Gold Rush, Frontier days, and man against the elements. London was himself a great adventurer, who put his experiences to use in novels such as *The Sea Wolf* and *The Call of the Wild*.

Here is Jack London at his best . . .

'Love of Life' (1905)
by Jack London

'This out of all will remain,
They have lived and have tossed,
So much of the game will be gain,
Though the gold of the dice has been lost.'

They limped painfully down the bank, and once the foremost of the two men staggered among the rough-strewn rocks. They were tired and weak, and their faces had the drawn expression of patience which comes of hardship long endured. They were heavily burdened with blanket packs which were strapped to their shoulders. Head-straps passing across the forehead helped to support these packs. Each man carried a rifle. They walked in a stooping posture, the shoulders well forward, the head still farther forward, the eyes bent upon the ground.

"I wish we had just about two of them cartridges that's layin' in that cache of ourn," said the second man.

His voice was utterly and drearily expressionless. He spoke without enthusiasm. But the first man, limping into the milky stream that foamed over the rocks, vouchsafed no reply.

The other man followed at his heels. They did not remove their footgear though the water was icy cold—so cold that their ankles ached and their feet went numb. In places the water dashed against their knees, and both men staggered for footing.

The man who followed slipped on a smooth boulder, nearly fell, but recovered himself with a violent effort, at the same time uttering a sharp exclamation of pain. He seemed faint and dizzy, and put out his free hand, while he reeled as though seeking support against the air. When he had steadied himself he stepped forward, but reeled again and nearly fell. Then he stood still and looked at the other man, who had never turned his head.

The man stood still for fully a minute, as though debating with himself. Then he called out—

"I say, Bill, I've sprained my ankle."

Bill staggered on through the milky water. He did not look round. The man watched him go, and though his face was expressionless as ever, his eyes were like the eyes of a wounded deer waiting the final slaughter.

The other man limped up the farther bank and continued straight on without looking back. The man in the stream watched him. His lips trembled a little, so that the rough thatch of brown hair which covered them was visibly agitated. His tongue even strayed out to moisten them.

"Bill!" he cried out.

It was the pleading cry of a strong man in distress, but Bill's head did not turn. The man watched him go, limping grotesquely and lurching forward with stammering gait up the slope toward the soft sky-line of the low-lying hill. He watched him go till he passed over the crest and disappeared. Then he turned his gaze and slowly took in the circle of the world that remained to him, now that Bill was gone.

Near the horizon the sun was smouldering dimly, almost obscured by formless mists and vapours which gave an impression of mass and density without outline or tangibility. The man pulled out his watch, the while resting his weight on one leg. It was four o'clock, and as the season was near the last of July or first of August—he did not know the precise date within a week or two—he knew that the sun roughly marked the north-west. He looked to the south and knew that somewhere beyond those bleak hills lay the Great Bear Lake; also, he knew that in that direction the Arctic Circle cut its forbidding way across the Canadian Barrens. This stream in which he stood was a feeder to the Coppermine River, which, in turn, flowed north and emptied into Coronation Gulf and the Arctic Ocean. He had never been there, but he had seen it once on a Hudson's Bay Company chart.

Again his gaze completed the circle of the world about him. It was not a heartening spectacle. Everywhere was soft sky-line. The hills were all low-lying. There were no trees, no shrubs, no grasses—naught but a tremendous and terrible desolation that sent fear swiftly dawning into his eyes.

"Bill!" he whispered, once, and twice—"Bill!"

He cowered in the midst of the milky water as though the vastness were pressing in upon him with overwhelming force, brutally crushing him with its complacent awfulness. He began to shake, as with an ague-fit, till the gun fell from his hand with a splash. This served to rouse him. He fought with his fear and pulled himself together, groping in the water and recovering the weapon. He hitched his pack farther over on his left shoulder, so as to take a portion of its weight off the injured ankle. Then he proceeded, slowly and carefully, wincing with pain, to the bank.

He did not stop. With a desperation that was madness, unmindful of the pain, he hurried up the slope to the crest of the hill over which his comrade had disappeared—more grotesque and comical by far than that limping, jerking comrade. But at the crest he saw a shallow valley, empty of life. He fought with his fear again, overcame it, hitched the pack still farther over on his left shoulder, and lurched on down the slope.

The bottom of the valley was soggy with water, which the thick moss held, sponge-like, close to the surface. This water squirted out from under his feet at every step, and each time he lifted a foot the action culminated in a sucking sound as the wet moss reluctantly released its grip. He picked his way from muskeg to muskeg, and followed the other man's footsteps along and across the rocky ledges which thrust like islets through the sea of moss.

Though alone, he was not lost. Farther on he knew he would come to where dead spruce and fir, very small and shrivelled, bordered the shore of a little lake, the *tit-chin-nichilie* in the tongue of the country, the 'land of little sticks'. And into that lake flowed a small stream, the water of which was not milky. There was rush-grass on that stream—this he remembered well—but no timber, and he would follow it till its first trickle ceased at a divide. He would cross this divide to the first trickle of another stream flowing to the west, which he would follow until it emptied into the River Dease; and here he would find a cache, under an upturned canoe and piled over with many rocks. And in this cache would be ammunition for his empty gun, fish-hooks and lines, a small net—all the utilities for the killing and snaring of food. Also, he would find flour—not much—a piece of bacon, and some beans.

Bill would be waiting for him there, and they would paddle away south, down the Dease to the Great Bear Lake. And south across the lake they would go, ever south, till they gained the Mackenzie. And south, still south, they would go—while the winter raced vainly after them, and the ice formed in the eddies, and the days grew chill and crisp—south to some warm Hudson's Bay Company post, where timber grew tall and generous and there was grub without end.

These were the thoughts of the man as he strove onward. But hard as he strove with his body, he strove equally hard with his mind, trying to think that Bill had not deserted him, that Bill would surely wait for him at the cache. He was compelled to think this thought, or else there would not be any use to strive, and he would have lain down and died. And as the dim ball of the sun sank slowly into the north-north-west, he covered every inch, and many times, of his and Bill's flight south before the down-coming winter. And he conned the grub of the cache and the grub of the Hudson's Bay Company post over and over again, this man, for he was very hungry. He had not eaten for two days; for a far longer time he had not had all he wanted to eat. Often he stooped and picked pale muskeg-berries, put them into his mouth, and chewed and swallowed them. A muskeg-berry is a bit of seed enclosed in a bit of water. In the mouth the water melts away and the seed chews sharp and bitter. The man knew there was no nourishment in the berries, but he chewed them patiently, with a hope greater than knowledge and defying experience.

At nine o'clock he stubbed his toe on a rocky ledge, and from sheer weariness and weakness staggered and fell. He lay for some time, without movement, on his side. Then he slipped out of the pack-straps and clumsily dragged himself into a sitting posture. It was not yet dark, and in the lingering twilight he groped about among the rocks for shreds of dry moss. When he had gathered a heap he built a fire—a smouldering, smudgy fire—and put a tin pot of water on to boil.

He unwrapped his pack, and the first thing he did was to count his matches. There were sixty-seven. He counted them three times to make sure. He divided them into several portions, wrapping them in oil-paper, disposing of one bunch in his empty tobacco-pouch, of another bunch in the inside band of his battered hat, of a third bunch under his shirt on the chest. This accomplished, a panic came upon him, and he unwrapped them all and counted them again. There were still sixty-seven.

He dried his wet foot-gear by the fire. The moccasins were in sodden shreds. The blanket socks were worn through in places, and his feet were raw and bleeding. His ankle was throbbing, and he gave it an examination. It had swollen to the size of his knee. He tore a long strip from one of his two blankets and bound the ankle tightly. He tore other strips and bound them about his feet to serve for both moccasins and socks. Then he drank the pot of water, steaming hot, wound his watch, and crawled between his blankets.

He slept like a dead man. The brief darkness around midnight came and went. The sun arose in the north-north-east—at least, the day dawned in that quarter, for the sun was hidden by grey clouds.

At six o'clock he awoke, quietly, lying on his back. He gazed straight up into the grey sky and knew that he was hungry. As he rolled over on his elbow he was startled by a loud snort, and saw a bull caribou regarding him with alert curiosity. The animal was not more than fifty feet away, and instantly into the man's mind leaped the vision and the savour of a caribou steak sizzling and frying over a fire. Mechanically he reached for the empty gun, drew a bead, and pulled the trigger. The bull snorted and leaped away, his hoofs rattling and clattering as he fled across the ledges.

The man cursed and flung the empty gun from him. He groaned aloud as he started to drag himself to his feet. It was a slow and arduous task. His joints were like rusty hinges.

They worked harshly in their sockets, with much friction, and each bending or unbending was accomplished only through a sheer exertion of will. When he finally gained his feet, another minute or so was consumed in straightening up so that he could stand erect as a man should stand.

He crawled up a small knoll and surveyed the prospect. There were no trees, no bushes, nothing but a grey sea of moss scarcely diversified by grey rocks, grey-coloured lakelets, and grey streamlets. The sky was grey. There was no sun or hint of sun. He had no idea of north, and he had forgotten the way he had come to this spot the night before. But he was not lost. He knew that. Soon he would come to the land of the little sticks. He felt that it lay off to the left, somewhere, not far, possibly just over the next low hill.

He went back to put his pack into shape for travelling. He assured himself of the existence of his three separate parcels of matches, though he did not stop to count them. But he did linger, debating over a squat moose-hide sack. It was not large. He could hide it under his two hands. He knew that it weighed fifteen pounds—as much as all the rest of the pack—and it worried him. He finally set it to one side and proceeded to roll the pack. He paused to gaze at the squat moose-hide sack. He picked it up hastily, with a defiant glance about him, as though the desolation were trying to rob him of it; and when he arose to his feet to stagger on into the day it was included in the pack on his back.

He bore away to the left, stopping now and again to eat muskeg-berries. His ankle had stiffened, his limp was more pronounced; but the pain of it was as nothing compared with the pain of his stomach. The hunger pangs were sharp. They gnawed and gnawed until he could not keep his mind steady on the course he must pursue to gain the land of little sticks. The muskeg-berries did not allay this gnawing, while they made his tongue and the roof of his month sore with their irritating bite.

He came upon a valley where rock ptarmigan rose on whirring wings from the ledges and muskegs. *Ker—ker—ker* was the cry they made. He threw stones at them, but could not hit them. He placed his pack on the ground and stalked them as a cat stalks a sparrow. The sharp rocks cut through the legs of his pants till his knees left a trail of blood. But the hurt was lost in the hurt of his hunger. He squirmed over the wet moss, saturating his clothes and chilling his body, but he was not aware of it, so great was his fever for food. And always the ptarmigan rose whirring before him, till their *ker—ker—ker* became a mock to him, and he cursed them and cried aloud at them with their own cry.

Once he crawled upon one that must have been asleep. He did not see it till it shot up in his face from its rocky nook. He made a clutch as startled as was the rise of the ptarmigan, and there remained in his hand three tail-feathers. As he watched its flight he hated it as though it had done him some terrible wrong. Then he returned and shouldered his pack.

As the day wore along he came into valleys or swales where game was more plentiful. A band of caribou passed by, twenty and odd animals, tantalisingly within rifle range. He felt a wild desire to run after them, a certitude that he could run them down. A black fox came toward him carrying a ptarmigan in his mouth. The man shouted. It was a fearful cry, but the fox, leaping away in fright, did not drop the ptarmigan.

Late in the afternoon he followed a stream, milky with lime, which ran through sparse patches of rush-grass. Grasping these rushes firmly near the root, he pulled up what resembled a young onion-sprout no larger than a shingle-nail. It was tender, and his teeth sank into it with a crunch that promised deliciously of food. But its fibres were tough. It was composed of stringy filaments, saturated with water like the berries, and devoid of nourishment. But he threw off his pack and went into the rush-grass on hands and knees, crunching and munching like some bovine creature.

He was very weary, and often wished to rest—to lie down and sleep; but he was continually driven on, not so much by his desire to gain the land of little sticks as by his hunger. He searched small ponds for frogs, and dug up the earth with his nails for worms, though he knew that neither frogs nor worms existed so far north. He looked into every pool of water vainly, until, as the long twilight came on, he discovered a solitary fish, the size of a minnow, in such a pool. He plunged his arm in up to the shoulder, but it eluded him. He reached for it with both hands, and stirred up the milky mud at the bottom. In his excitement he fell in, wetting himself to the waist. Then the water was too muddy to admit of his seeing the fish, and he was compelled to wait until the sediment had settled.

The pursuit was renewed till the water was again muddied. But he could not wait. He unstrapped the tin bucket and began to bale the pool. He baled wildly at first, splashing himself and flinging the water so short a distance that it ran back into the pool. He worked more carefully, striving to be cool, though his heart was pounding against his chest and his hands were trembling. At the end of half an hour the pool was nearly dry, not a cupful of water remained, and there was no fish. He found a hidden crevice among the stones through which it had escaped to the adjoining and larger pool—a pool which he could not empty in a night and a day. Had he known of the crevice he could have closed it with a rock at the beginning, and the fish would have been his.

Thus he thought, and crumpled up and sank down upon the wet earth. At first he cried softly, to himself, then he cried loudly, to the pitiless desolation that ringed him around; and for a long time after he was shaken by great dry sobs.

He built a fire and warmed himself by drinking quarts of hot water, and made camp on a rocky ledge in the same fashion he had the night before. The last thing he did was to see that his matches were dry and to wind his watch. The blankets were wet and clammy. His ankle pulsed with pain. But he knew only that he was hungry, and through his restless sleep he dreamed of feasts and banquets and of food served and spread in all imaginable ways.

He awoke, chilled and sick. There was no sun. The grey of earth and sky had become deeper, more profound. A raw wind was blowing, and the first flurries of snow were whitening the hill-tops. The air about him thickened and grew white while he made a fire and boiled more water. It was wet snow, half rain, and the flakes were large. At first they melted as soon as they came in contact with the earth, but more ever fell, covering the ground, putting out the fire, spoiling his supply of moss-fuel.

This was the signal for him to strap on his pack and stumble onward, he knew not where. He was not concerned with the land of little sticks, nor with Bill and the cache under the upturned canoe by the River Dease. He was mastered by the verb 'to eat'. He was hunger-mad. He took no heed of the course he pursued, so long as that course led him through the swale bottoms. He felt his way through the wet snow to the watery muskeg-berries, and went by feel as he pulled up the rush-grass by the roots. But it was tasteless stuff and did not satisfy. He found a weed that tasted sour, and he ate all he could find of it, which was not much, for it was a creeping growth, easily hidden under the several inches of snow.

He had no fire that night, nor hot water, and crawled under his blanket to sleep the broken hunger-sleep. The snow turned into a cold rain. He awakened many times to feel it falling on his upturned face. Day came—a grey day and no sun. It had ceased raining. The keenness of his hunger had departed. Sensibility, so far as concerned the yearning for food, had been exhausted. There was a dull, heavy ache in his stomach, but it did not bother him so much. He was more rational, and once more he was chiefly interested in the land of little sticks and the cache by the River Dease.

He ripped the remnant of one of his blankets into strips and bound his bleeding feet. Also, he re-cinched the injured ankle and prepared himself for a day of travel. When he came to his pack he paused long over the squat moose-hide sack, but in the end it went with him.

The snow had melted under the rain, and only the hill-tops showed white. The sun came out, and he succeeded in locating the points of the compass, though he knew now that he was lost. Perhaps, in his previous days' wanderings, he had edged away too far to the left. He now bore off to the right to counteract the possible deviation from his true course.

Though the hunger pangs were no longer so exquisite, he realised that he was weak. He was compelled to pause for frequent rests when he attacked the muskeg-berries and rush-grass patches. His tongue felt dry and large, as though covered with a fine hairy growth, and it tasted bitter in his mouth. His heart gave him a great deal of trouble. When he had travelled a few minutes it would begin a remorseless thump, thump, thump, and then leap up and away in a painful flutter of beats that choked him and made him go faint and dizzy.

In the middle of the day he found two minnows in a large pool. It was impossible to bale it, but he was calmer now and managed to catch them in his tin bucket. They were no longer than his little finger, but he was not particularly hungry. The dull ache in his stomach had been growing duller and fainter. It seemed almost that his stomach was dozing. He ate the fish raw, masticating with painstaking care, for the eating was a pure act of reason. While he had no desire to eat, be knew that he must eat to live.

In the evening he caught three more minnows, eating two and saving the third for breakfast. The sun had dried stray shreds of moss, and he was able to warm himself with hot water. He had not covered more than ten miles that day, and the next day, travelling whenever his heart permitted him, he covered no more than five miles. But his stomach did not give him the slightest uneasiness. It had gone to sleep. He was in a strange country, too, and the caribou were growing more plentiful, also the wolves. Often their yelps drifted across the desolation, and once he saw three of them slinking away before his path.

Another night, and in the morning, being more rational, he untied the leather string that fastened the squat moosehide sack. From its open mouth poured a yellow stream of coarse gold-dust and nuggets. He roughly divided the gold in halves, caching one half on a prominent ledge, wrapped in a piece of blanket, and returning the other half to the sack. He also began to use strips of the one remaining blanket for his feet. He still clung to his gun, for there were cartridges in that cache by the River Dease.

This was a day of fog, and this day hunger awoke in him again. He was very weak, and was afflicted with a giddiness which at times blinded him. It was no uncommon thing now to stumble and fall; and stumbling once, he fell squarely into a ptarmigan nest. There were four newly-hatched chicks, a day old, little specks of pulsating life, no more than a mouthful, and he ate them, ravenously, thrusting them alive into his mouth and crunching them like egg-shells between his teeth. The mother ptarmigan beat about him with great outcry. He used his gun as a club with which to knock her over, but she dodged out of reach. He threw stones at her, and with one chance shot broke a wing. Then she fluttered away, running, trailing the broken wing, with him in pursuit.

The little chicks had no more than whetted his appetite. He hopped and bobbed clumsily along on his injured ankle, throwing stones and screaming hoarsely at times; at other times hopping and bobbing silently along, picking himself up grimly and patiently when he fell, or rubbing his eyes with his hand when the giddiness threatened to overpower him.

The chase led him across swampy ground in the bottom of the valley, and he came upon footprints in the moss. They were not his own—he could see that. They must be Bill's. But he could not stop, for the mother ptarmigan was running on. He would catch her first, then he would return and investigate.

He exhausted the mother ptarmigan; but he exhausted himself. She lay panting on her side, He lay panting on his side, a dozen feet away, unable to crawl to her. And as he recovered, she recovered, fluttering out of reach as his hungry hand went out to her. The chase was resumed. Night settled down, and she escaped. He stumbled from weakness and pitched headforemost on his face, cutting his cheek, his pack upon his back. He did not move for a long while; then he rolled over on his side, wound his watch, and lay there until morning.

Another day of fog. Half of his last blanket had gone into foot-wrappings. He failed to pick up Bill's trail. It did not matter. His hunger was driving him too compellingly . . . only . . . only he wondered if Bill, too, were lost. By midday the irk of his pack became too oppressive. Again he divided the gold, this time merely spilling half of it on the ground. In the afternoon he threw the rest of it away, there remaining to him only the half-blanket, the tin bucket, and the rifle.

A hallucination began to trouble him. He felt confident that one cartridge remained to him. It was in the chamber of the rifle, and he had overlooked it. On the other hand, he knew all the time that the chamber was empty. But the hallucination persisted. He fought it off for hours, then threw his rifle open and was confronted with emptiness. The disappointment was as bitter as though he had really expected to find the cartridge.

He plodded on for half an hour, when the hallucination arose again. Again he fought it, and still it persisted, till for very relief he opened his rifle to unconvince himself. At times his mind wandered farther afield, and he plodded on, a mere automaton, strange conceits and whimsicalities gnawing at his brain like worms. But these excursions out of the real were of brief duration, for ever the pangs of the hunger-bite called him back. He was jerked back abruptly, once, from such an excursion, by a sight that caused him nearly to faint. He reeled and swayed, doddering like a drunken man to keep from falling. Before him stood a horse. A horse! He could not believe his eyes. A thick mist was in them, intershot with sparkling points of light. He rubbed his eyes savagely to clear his vision, and beheld, not a horse, but a great brown bear. The animal was studying him with bellicose curiosity.

The man had brought his gun half way to his shoulder before he realised. He lowered it, and drew his hunting-knife from its beaded sheath at his hip. Before him was meat and life. He ran his thumb along the edge of his knife. It was sharp; the point was sharp. He would fling himself upon the bear and kill it. But his heart began its warning thump, thump, thump. Then followed the wild upward leap and tattoo of flutters, the pressing as of an iron band about his forehead, the creeping of the dizziness into his brain.

His desperate courage was evicted by a great surge of fear. In his weakness, what if the animal attacked him! He drew himself up to his most imposing stature, gripping the knife and staring hard at the bear. The bear advanced clumsily a couple of steps, reared up, and gave vent to a tentative growl. If the man ran, he would run after him. But the man did not run. He was animated now with the courage of fear, the courage of the cornered rat. He, too, growled—savagely, terribly, voicing the fear that is to life germane, and that lies twisted about life's deepest roots.

The bear edged away to one side, growling menacingly, himself appalled by this mysterious creature that appeared upright and unafraid. But the man did not move. He stood like a statue till the danger was past, when he yielded to a fit of trembling and sank down into the wet moss.

He pulled himself together and went on, afraid now in a new way. It was not the fear that he should die passively from lack of food, but that he should be destroyed violently before starvation had exhausted the last particle of the endeavour in him that made toward surviving. There were the wolves. Back and forth across the desolation drifted their howls, weaving the very air into a fabric of menace that was so tangible that he found himself, arms in the air, pressing it back from him as it might be the walls of a wind-blown tent.

Now and again the wolves, in packs of two and three, crossed his path. But they sheered clear of him. They were not in sufficient numbers; and, besides, they were hunting the caribou, which did not battle, while this strange creature that walked erect might scratch and bite.

In the late afternoon he came upon scattered bones where the wolves had made a kill. The debris had been a caribou calf an hour before, squawking and running and very much alive. He contemplated the bones, clean-picked and polished, pink with the cell-life in them which had not yet died. Could it possibly be that he might be that ere the day was done? Such was life, eh? A vain and fleeting thing. It was only life that pained. There was no hurt in death. To die was to sleep. It meant cessation, rest. Then why was he not content to die?

But he did not moralise long. He was squatting in the moss, a bone in his mouth, sucking at the shreds of life that still dyed it faintly pink. The sweet meaty taste, thin and elusive almost as a memory, maddened him. He closed his jaws on the bones and crunched. Sometimes it was the bone that broke, sometimes his teeth. Then he crushed the bones between rocks, pounded them to a pulp, and swallowed them. He pounded his fingers, too, in his haste, and yet found a moment in which to feel surprise at the fact that his fingers did not hurt much when caught under the descending rock.

Came two frightful days of snow and rain. He did not know when he made camp, when he broke camp. He travelled in the night as much as in the day. He rested wherever he fell, crawled on whenever the dying life in him flickered up and burned less dimly. He, as a man, no longer strove. It was the life in him, unwilling to die, that drove him on. He did not suffer. His nerves had become blunted, numb, while his mind was filled with weird visions and delicious dreams.

But ever he sucked and chewed on the crushed bones of the caribou calf, the least remnants of which he had gathered up and carried with him. He crossed no more hills or divides, but automatically followed a large stream which flowed through a wide and shallow valley. He did not see this stream, or this valley. He saw nothing save visions. Soul and body walked or crawled side by side, yet apart, so slender was the thread that bound them.

He awoke, in his right mind, lying on his back on a rocky ledge. The sun was shining bright and warm. Afar off he heard the squawking of caribou calves. He was aware of vague memories of rain, and wind, and snow, but whether he had been beaten by the storm for two days or two weeks he did not know.

For some time he lay without movement, the genial sunshine pouring upon him, and saturating his miserable body with its warmth. A fine day, he thought. Perhaps he could manage to locate himself. By a painful effort he rolled over on his side. Below him flowed a wide and sluggish river. Its unfamiliarity puzzled him. Slowly he followed it with his eyes, winding in wide sweeps among the bleak, bare hills, bleaker and barer, and lower-lying than any hills he had yet encountered. Slowly, deliberately, without excitement or more than the most casual interest, he followed the course of the strange stream toward the sky-line, and saw it emptying into a bright and shining sea. He was still unexcited. Most unusual, he thought, a vision or a mirage—more likely a vision, a trick of his disordered mind. He was confirmed in this by sight of a ship lying at anchor in the midst of the shining sea. He closed his eyes for a while, then opened them. Strange how the vision persisted. Yet not strange. He knew there were no seas or ships in the heart of the Barren-lands, just as he had known there was no cartridge in the empty rifle.

He heard a snuffle behind him, a half-choking gasp or cough. Very slowly, because of his exceeding weakness and stiffness, he rolled over on his other side. He could see nothing near at hand, but he waited patiently. Again came the snuffle and cough, and, outlined between two jagged rocks, not a score of feet away, he made out the grey head of a wolf. The sharp ears were not pricked so sharply as he had seen them on other wolves, the eyes were bleared and bloodshot, the head seemed to droop limply and forlornly. The animal blinked continually in the sunshine. It seemed sick. As he looked, it snuffled and coughed again.

This, at least, was real, he thought, and turned on the other side so that he might see the reality of the world which had been veiled from him before by the vision. But the sea still shone in the distance, and the ship's spars were plainly discernible. Was it reality after all? He closed his eyes for a long while, and thought, and then it came to him. He had been making north by east, away from the Dease Divide, and into the Coppermine Valley. This wide and sluggish river was the Coppermine. That shining sea was the Arctic Ocean. That ship was a whaler, strayed east, far east, from the mouth of the Mackenzie, and it was lying at anchor in Coronation Gulf. He remembered the Hudson's Bay Company chart he had seen long ago, and it was all clear and reasonable to him.

He sat up and turned his attention to immediate affairs. He had worn through the blanket-wrappings, and his feet were like shapeless lumps of raw meat. His last blanket was gone. Rifle and knife were both missing. He had lost his hat somewhere, with the bunch of matches in the band, but the matches against his chest were safe and dry inside the tobacco-pouch and oil-paper. He looked at his watch. It marked eleven o'clock, and was still running. Evidently he had kept it wound.

He was calm and collected. Though extremely weak, he had no sensation of pain. He was not hungry. The thought of food was not even pleasant to him, and whatever he did was done by his reason alone. He ripped off the legs of his pants to the knees, and bound them about his feet. Somehow he had succeeded in retaining the tin bucket. He would have some hot water before he began what he foresaw was to be a terrible journey to the ship.

His movements were slow. He shook as with a palsy. When he started to collect dry moss he found he could not rise to his feet. He tried again and again, then contented himself with crawling about on hands and knees. Once he crawled near to the sick wolf. The animal dragged itself reluctantly out of his way, licking its chops with a tongue which seemed hardly to have the strength to curl. The man noticed that the tongue was not the customary healthful red. It was a yellowish brown, and seemed coated with a rough and half-dry mucus.

After he had drunk a quart of hot water, the man found he was able to stand, and even to walk as well as a dying man might be supposed to walk. Every minute or so he was compelled to rest. His steps were feeble and uncertain, just as the wolf's that trailed him were feeble and uncertain; and that night, when the shining sea was blotted out by blackness, he knew he was nearer to it by no more than four miles.

Throughout the night he heard the cough of the sick wolf, and now and then the squawking of the caribou calves. There was life all around him; but it was strong life, very much alive and well, and he knew the sick wolf clung to the sick man's trail in the hope that the man would die first. In the morning, on first opening his eyes, he beheld it regarding him with a wistful and hungry stare. It stood crouched, with tail between its legs, like a miserable and woe-begone dog. It shivered in the chill morning wind, and grinned dispiritedly when the man spoke to it in a voice which achieved no more than a hoarse whisper.

The sun rose brightly, and all morning the man tottered and fell toward the ship on the shining sea. The weather was perfect. It was the brief Indian summer of the high latitudes. It might last a week. Tomorrow or next day it might be gone.

In the afternoon the man came upon a trail. It was of another man who did not walk, but who dragged himself on all-fours. The man thought it might be Bill, but he thought in a dull uninterested way. He had no curiosity. In fact, sensation and emotion had left him. He was no longer susceptible to pain. Stomach and nerves had gone to sleep. Yet the life that was in him drove him on. He was very weary, but it refused to die. It was because it refused to die that he still ate muskeg-berries and minnows, drank his hot water, and kept a wary eye on the sick wolf.

He followed the trail of the other man who dragged himself along, and soon came to the end of it—a few fresh-picked bones where the moss was marked by the footpads of many wolves. He saw a squat moose-hide sack, mate to his own, which had been torn by sharp teeth. He picked it up, though its weight was almost too much for his feeble fingers. Bill had carried it to the last. Ha! ha! he would have the laugh on Bill. He would himself survive and carry it to the ship in the shining sea. His mirth was hoarse and ghastly, like a raven's croak, and the sick wolf joined him, howling lugubriously. The man ceased suddenly. How could he have the laugh on Bill if that were Bill—if those bones, so pinky-white and clean, were Bill!

He turned away. Well, Bill had deserted him; but he would not take the gold, nor would he suck Bill's bones.

Bill would have, though, had it been the other way round, he mused as he staggered on.

He came to a pool of water. Stooping over in quest of minnows, he jerked his head back as though he had been stung. He had caught sight of his reflected face. So horrible was it that sensibility awoke long enough to be shocked. There were three minnows in the pool, which was too large to drain, and after several ineffectual attempts to catch them in the tin bucket he forbore. He was afraid, because of his great weakness, that he might fall in and drown. It was for this reason that he did not trust himself to the river astride one of the many drift-logs which lined its sand-spits.

That day he decreased the distance between him and the ship by three miles, the next day by two—for he was crawling now, as Bill had crawled—and the end of the fifth day found the ship still seven miles away, and him unable to make even a mile a day. Still the Indian summer held on, and he continued to crawl and faint turn and turn about, and ever the sick wolf coughed and wheezed at his heels. His knees had become raw meat like his feet, and though he padded them with the shirt from his back, it was a red track he left behind him on the moss and stones. Once, glancing back, he saw the wolf licking hungrily his bleeding trail, and he saw sharply what his own end might be . . . unless . . . unless he could get the wolf. Then began as grim a tragedy of existence as was ever played—a sick man that crawled, a sick wolf that limped, two creatures dragging their dying carcasses across the desolation and hunting each other's lives.

Had it been a well wolf it would not have mattered so much to the man, but the thought of going to feed the maw of that loathsome and all but dead thing was repugnant to him. He was finicky. His mind had begun to wander again and to be perplexed by hallucinations, while his lucid intervals grew rarer and shorter.

He was awakened once, from a faint, by a wheeze close in his ear. The wolf leaped lamely back, losing its footing and falling in its weakness. It was ludicrous, but he was not amused. Nor was he even afraid. He was too far gone for that. But his mind was for the moment clear, and he lay and considered. The ship was no more than four miles away. He could see it quite distinctly when he rubbed the mists out of his eyes, and he could see the white sail of a small boat cutting the water of the shining sea. But he could never crawl those four miles. He knew that, and was very calm in the knowledge. He knew that he could not crawl half a mile. And yet he wanted to live. It was unreasonable that he should die after all he had undergone. Fate asked too much of him. And, dying, he declined to

Ruskin Bond

die. It was stark madness, perhaps, but in the very grip of death he defied death and refused to die.

He closed his eyes and composed himself with infinite precaution. He steeled himself to keep above the suffocating languor that lapped like a rising tide through all the wells of his being. It was very like a sea, this deadly languor, that rose and rose and drowned his consciousness bit by bit. Sometimes he was all but submerged, swimming through oblivion with a faltering stroke; and again, by some strange alchemy of soul, he would find another shred of will and strike out more strongly again.

Without movement he lay on his back, and he could hear, slowly drawing nearer and nearer, the wheezing intake and output of the sick wolf's breath. It drew closer, ever closer, through an infinitude of time, and he did not move. It was at his ear. The harsh, dry tongue grated like sandpaper against his cheek. His hands shot out—or at least he willed them to shoot out. The fingers were curved like talons, but they closed on empty air. Swiftness and certitude require strength, and the man had not this strength.

The patience of the wolf was terrible. The man's patience was no less terrible. For half a day he lay motionless, fighting off unconsciousness, and waiting for the thing that was to feed upon him and upon which he wished to feed. Sometimes the languid sea rose over him and he dreamed long dreams, but ever through it all, waking and dreaming, he waited for the wheezing breath and the harsh caress of the tongue.

He did not hear the breath, and he slipped slowly from some dream to the feel of the tongue along his hand. He waited. The fangs pressed softly, the pressure increased, the wolf was exerting its last strength in an effort to sink teeth in the food for which it had waited so long. But the man had waited long, and the lacerated hand closed on the jaw. Slowly, while the wolf struggled feebly and the hand clutched feebly, the other hand crept across to grip. Five minutes later the whole weight of the man's body was on top of the wolf. The hands had not sufficient strength to choke the animal, but the face of the man was pressed close to the throat of the wolf, and the mouth was full of hair. At the end of half an hour the man was aware of a warm trickle in his throat. It was not pleasant. It was like molten lead being forced into his stomach, but it was forced by his will alone. Later, the man rolled over on his back and slept.

There were some members of a scientific expedition on the whaleship *Bedford*. From the deck they remarked a strange object on the shore. It was moving down the beach toward the water. They were unable to classify it, and, being scientific men, they climbed into the whaleboat alongside and went ashore to see. And they saw something that was alive but that could hardly be called a man. It was blind, unconscious. It squirmed along the ground like some monstrous worm. Most of its efforts were ineffectual, but it was persistent, and it writhed and twisted and went ahead perhaps a score of feet an hour.

Three weeks afterward the man lay in a bunk on the whaleship *Bedford*, and, with tears streaming down his wasted cheeks, told who he was and what he had undergone. He also babbled incoherently of his mother, of sunny Southern California, and a home among the orange-groves and flowers.

The days were not many after that when he sat at table with the scientific men and ship's officers. He gloated over the spectacle of so much food, watching it anxiously as it went into the mouths of others. With the disappearance of each mouthful an expression of deep regret came into his eyes. He was quite sane, yet he hated these men at mealtime because they ate so much food. He was haunted by a fear that it would not last. He inquired of the cook, the cabin boy, the captain, concerning the food stores. They reassured him countless times, but he could not believe them, and pried cunningly about the lazaretto to see with his own eyes.

It was noticed that the man was getting fat. He grew stouter with each day. The scientific men shook their heads and theorized. They limited the man at his meals, but still his girth increased, and his body swelled prodigiously under his shirt.

The sailors grinned. They knew. And when the scientific men set a watch on the man, they knew too. They saw him slouch for'ard after breakfast, and, like a mendicant with outstretched palm, accost a sailor. The sailor grinned and passed him a fragment of sea biscuit. He clutched it avariciously, looked at it as a miser looks at gold, and thrust it into his shirt-bosom. Similar were the donations from other grinning sailors.

The scientific men were discreet. They left him alone. But they privily examined his bunk. It was lined with hardtack; the mattress was stuffed with hardtack; every nook and cranny was filled to overflowing with hardtack. Yet he was sane. He was taking precautions against another possible famine, that was all. He would recover from it, the scientific men said; and he did, ere the *Bedford's* anchor rumbled down in San Francisco Bay.

(As published in *Blackwood's Magazine*, December 1905.)

7

Bicycle Days

I was twelve when I was given my first bicycle, and within a week I had fallen off and broken my arm. Badly set by a Dehradun doctor, my left arm remained bent, enabling me to bowl left arm off-breaks which turn out to be leg-breaks to right-handed batsmen and off-breaks to left-handed batsmen. Does that make sense? I suppose not. But cricket never did make much sense.

Anyway, the 1950s was the Bicycle Age in small-town India, and across the country bicycles far outnumbered cars and pony-drawn tongas. Today, cyclists have a hard time getting anywhere with any degree of safety, being continually bullied and buffeted around by cars, buses, trucks and motorcycles. In Europe, however, the bicycle is making something of a comeback. You get some exercise, you save on petrol, you can take by-lanes and shortcuts and avoid time-consuming traffic jams.

In the early years of the twentieth century the bicycle was the most popular means of both recreation and transportation. It is central to many great works of literature, including Jerome K. Jerome's *Three Men on the Bummel*, the sequel to *Three Men in a Boat*; William Saroyan's *The Bicycle Rider in Beverly Hills*; and several works by H.G. Wells, including *The Wheels of Chance* and *The History of Mr. Polly*.

Wells came from a very humble background. His father kept a small hardware shop; his mother worked as a domestic servant. He educated himself, won a scholarship to the Imperial College of Science and became a schoolteacher and biology tutor. In 1893 he published his first book—a two-volume *Text-book of Biology*.

He went on to become one of the twentieth century's most successful and influential writers, producing well over one hundred works of fiction, science fiction, history, sociology, political commentary, autobiography and prophecy.

Wells was a pioneer of science fiction (*The Invisible Man*, *The War of the Worlds*, *The First Men on the Moon* to name just a few); a novelist of ideas and originality (*The Passionate Friends*, *Tono Bungay*, *Ann Veronica*, *The World of William Clissold*); works of humour and observation (*Kipps*, *The History of Mr Polly*, *Love and Mr. Lewisham*); history (*The Outline of History*, *Russia in the Shadows*, *War and the Future*); autobiography (*Mind at the End of its Tether*) and many essays, short stories, film stories and educational texts.

The History of Mr Polly (1910) is probably his most loved and enduring work of fiction—a comic novel, and an oddly moving one, in which the central characters represent both the individual and the universal.

Mr Polly is a shopkeeper in a small English seaside town. Frustrated and bankrupt, he sets fire to his shop and takes off on his bicycle in search of romance, adventure and happiness.

Like Mr Polly, I have, on several occasions in the course of a long life, given up a good job and a steady income and ventured into unknown territory, the uncertainties of full-time writing. Romance and adventure are easily found if you go looking for them. Happiness is something else. Just when you think you have found it, the gods grow jealous and snatch it away!

In this episode Mr Polly falls in love. You will have to read the book to find out whether it brings him happiness.

From *The History of Mr Polly* (1910)
by H.G. Wells

Romance

And now Mr Polly began to lead a double life. With the Johnsons he professed to be inclined, but not so conclusively inclined as to be inconvenient, to get a shop for himself—to be, to use the phrase he preferred, 'looking for an opening'. He would ride off in the afternoon upon that research, remarking that he was going to 'cast a strategical eye' on Chertsey or Weybridge. But if not all roads, still a great majority of them led by however devious ways to Stamton, and to laughter and increasing familiarity. Relations developed with Annie and Minnie and Miriam. Their various characters were increasingly interesting. The laughter became perceptibly less abundant, something of the fizz had gone from the first opening, still these visits remained wonderfully friendly and upholding. Then back he would come to grave but evasive discussions with Johnson.

Johnson was really anxious to get Mr Polly 'into something'. His was a reserved, honest character, and he would really have preferred to see his lodger doing things for himself than receive his money for housekeeping. He hated waste, anybody's waste, much more than he desired profit. But Mrs Johnson was all for Mr Polly's loitering. She seemed much the more human and likeable of the two to Mr Polly.

He tried at times to work up enthusiasm for the various avenues to well-being his discussion with Johnson opened. But they remained disheartening prospects. He imagined himself wonderfully smartened up, acquiring style and value in a London shop; but the picture was stiff and unconvincing. He tried to rouse himself to enthusiasm by the idea of his property increasing by leaps and bounds, by twenty pounds a year or so, let us say, each year, in a well-placed little shop, the corner shop Johnson favoured. There was a certain picturesque interest in imagining cut-throat economies, but his heart told him there would be little in practising them.

And then it happened to Mr Polly that real Romance came out of dreamland into his life, intoxicated and gladdened him with sweetly beautiful suggestions—and left him. She came and left him as that dear lady leaves so many of us, alas! not sparing him one jot or one tittle of the hollowness of her retreating aspect.

It was all the more to Mr Polly's taste that the thing should happen as things happen in books.

In a resolute attempt not to get to Stamton that day, he had turned due southward from Easewood towards a country where the abundance of bracken jungles, lady's smock, stitchwort, bluebells, and grassy stretches by the wayside under shady trees does much to compensate the lighter type of mind for the absence of promising 'openings'. He turned aside from the road, wheeled his machine along a faintly marked attractive trail through bracken until he came to a heap of logs against a high old stone wall with a damaged coping and wallflower plants already gone to seed. He sat down, balanced the straw hat on a convenient lump of wood, lit a cigarette, and abandoned himself to agreeable musings and the friendly observation of a cheerful little brown and grey bird his stillness presently encouraged to approach him.

'This is All Right,' said Mr Polly softly to the little brown and grey bird. 'Business—later.'

He reflected that he might go on this way for four or five years, and then be scarcely worse off than he had been in his father's lifetime.

'Vile Business,' said Mr Polly.

Then Romance appeared. Or to be exact, Romance became audible.

Romance began as a series of small but increasingly vigorous movements on the other side of the wall, then as a voice murmuring, then as a falling of little fragments on the other side and as ten pink finger-tips, scarcely apprehended before Romance became startlingly and emphatically a leg, remained for a time a fine, slender, actively struggling limb, brown stockinged, and wearing a brown toe-worn shoe, and then . . . A handsome, red-haired girl wearing a short dress of blue linen was sitting astride the wall, panting, considerably disarranged by her climbing, and as yet unaware of Mr Polly . . .

His fine instincts made him turn his head away and assume an attitude of negligent contemplation, with his ears and mind alive to every sound behind him.

'Goodness!' said a voice, with a sharp note of surprise.

Mr Polly was on his feet in an instant. 'Dear me! Can I be of any assistance?' he said, with deferential gallantry.

'I don't know,' said the young lady, and regarded him calmly with clear blue eyes. 'I didn't know there was anyone here,' she added.

'Sorry,' said Mr Polly, 'if I am intrudacious. I didn't know you didn't want me to be here.'

She reflected for a moment on the word.

'It isn't that,' she said, surveying him. 'I oughtn't to get over the wall,' she explained. 'It's out of bounds; at least in term time. But this being holidays—'

Her manner placed the matter before him.

'Holidays is different,' said Mr Polly.

'I don't want to actually *break* the rules,' she said.

'Leave them behind you,' said Mr Polly, with a catch of the breath, 'where they are safe.' And marvelling at his own wit and daring, and indeed trembling within himself, he held out a hand for her.

She brought another brown leg from the unknown, and arranged her skirt with a dexterity altogether feminine.

'I think I'll stay on the wall,' she decided. 'So long as some of me's in bounds—'

She continued to regard him with an irresistible smile of satisfaction. Mr Polly smiled in return.

'You bicycle?' she said.

Mr Polly admitted the fact, and she said she did too

'All *my* people are in India,' she explained. 'It's beastly rot—I mean it's frightfully dull being left here alone.'

'All my people,' said Mr Polly, 'are in Heaven!'

'I say!'

'Fact,' said Mr Polly. 'Got nobody.'

'And that's why—' She checked her artless comment on his mourning. 'I say,' she said in a sympathetic voice, 'I *am* sorry. I really am. Was it a fire, or a ship—or something?'

Her sympathy was very delightful. He shook his head. 'The ordinary tables of mortality,' he said. 'First one, and then another.'

Behind his outward melancholy, delight was dancing wildly.

'Are *you* lonely?' asked the girl.

Mr Polly nodded.

'I was just sitting there in melancholic rectrospectatiousness,' he said, indicating the logs; and again a swift thoughtfulness swept across her face.

'There's no harm in our talking,' she reflected.

'It's a kindness. Won't you get down?'

She reflected, and surveyed the turf below and the scene around, and him.

'I'll stay on the wall,' she said, 'if only for bounds' sake.'

She certainly looked quite adorable on the wall. She had a fine neck and pointed chin that was particularly admirable from below, and pretty eyes and fine eyebrows are never so pretty as when they look down upon one. But no calculation of that sort, thank Heaven, was going on beneath her ruddy shock of hair.

*

'Let's talk,' she said, and for a time they were both tongue-tied.

Mr Polly's literary proclivities had taught him that under such circumstances a strain of gallantry was demanded. And something in his blood repeated that lesson.

'You make me feel like one of those old knights,' he said, 'who rode about the country looking for dragons and beautiful maidens and chivalresque adventures.'

'Oh!' she said. 'Why?'

'Beautiful maiden,' he said.

She flushed under her freckles with the quick bright flush those pretty red-haired people have. 'Nonsense!' she said.

'You are. I'm not the first to tell you that. A beautiful maiden imprisoned in an enchanted school.'

'*You* wouldn't think it enchanted.'

'And here am I—clad in steel. Well, not exactly, but my fiery war-horse is, anyhow. Ready to absquatulate all the dragons, and rescue you.'

She laughed, a jolly laugh, that showed delightfully gleaming teeth. 'I wish you could *see* the dragons,' she said, with great enjoyment. Mr Polly felt they were a sun's distance from the world of every day.

'Fly with me!' he dared.

She stared for a moment, and then went off into peals of laughter. 'You *are* funny!' she said, 'Why, I haven't known you five minutes.'

'One doesn't—in this mediaeval world. My mind is made up, anyhow.'

He was proud and pleased with his joke, and quick to change his key neatly. 'I wish one could,' he said.

'I wonder if people ever did.'

'If there were people like you.'

'We don't even know each other's names,' she remarked, with a descent to matters of fact.

'Yours is the prettiest name in the world.'

'How do you know?'

'It must be—anyhow.'

'It *is* rather pretty, you know. It's Christabel.'

'What did I tell you?'

'And yours?'

'Poorer than I deserve. It's Alfred.'

'*I* can't call you Alfred.'

'Well, Polly.'

'It's a girl's name!'

For a moment he went out of tune. 'I wish it was,' he said, and could have bitten out his tongue at the Larkins sound of it.

'I shan't forget it,' she remarked consolingly.

'I say,' she said, in the pause that followed, 'why are you riding about the country on a bicycle?'

'I'm doing it because I like it.'

She sought to estimate his social status on her limited basis of experience. He stood leaning with one hand against the wall, looking up at her and tingling with daring thoughts. He was a littleish man, you must remember, but neither mean-looking nor unhandsome in those days, sunburnt by his holiday and now warmly flushed. He had an inspiration to simple speech that no practised trifler with love could have bettered. 'There *is* love at first sight,' he said, and said it sincerely.

She stared at him with eyes round and big with excitement.

'I think,' she said slowly, and without any signs of fear or retreat, 'I ought to get back over the wall.'

'It needn't matter to you,' he said; 'I'm just a nobody. But I know you are the best and most beautiful thing I've ever spoken to.' His breath caught against something. 'No harm in telling you that,' he said.

'I should have to go back if I thought you were serious,' she said after a pause, and they both smiled together.

After that they talked in a fragmentary way for some time. The blue eyes surveyed Mr Polly with kindly curiosity from under a broad, finely-modelled brow, much as an exceptionally intelligent cat might survey a new sort of dog. She meant to find out all about him. She asked questions that riddled the honest knight in armour below, and probed even nearer to the hateful secret of the shop and his normal servitude. And when he made a flourish and mispronounced a word, a thoughtful shade passed like the shadow of a cloud across her face.

'Booom!' came the sound of a gong.

'Lordy!' cried the girl, and flashed a pair of brown legs at him and was gone.

Then her pink finger-tips reappeared, and the top of her red hair. 'Knight,' she cried from the other side of the wall. 'Knight there!'

'Lady!' he answered.

'Come again tomorrow.'

'At your command. But—'

'Yes?'

'Just one finger.'

'What do you mean?'

'To kiss.'

The rustle of retreating footsteps and silence . . .

But after he had waited next day for twenty minutes she reappeared, a little out of breath with the effort to surmount the wall, and head first this time. And it seemed to him she was lighter and more daring and altogether prettier than the dreams and enchanted memories that had filled the interval.

8

A Room of my Own

The roof and ceiling of my little room leaked badly, but at least it was my own room and I had it to myself most of the time; for it was at the far end of a queerly shaped cottage just off Dehra's Eastern Canal Road, recently taken on rent by my mother and stepfather.

It was the winter of 1948–49. My fourth winter holiday down from my boarding school in Simla, and the fourth house we'd moved into during that period. As usual, my stepfather's car business wasn't doing too well, and there were always problems with landlords, overdue rent, tax collectors, unpaid bills, etc. Our latest dwelling was badly in need of repairs, and somehow I knew we wouldn't be there long enough to see them being done.

My winter holidays lasted three months, and I spent most of my time reading, listening to the radio, or going for lonely bicycle rides. I did not know any other boys then. My grandmother's house, inherited by an aunt, was in the process of being sold, and I did not go there often; but the previous year, on a brief visit, I had discovered a set of Dickens in an old cupboard and I had appropriated

it, certain that if I did not do so it would be sold to the junk dealer along with other unwanted household bric-a-brac.

The books I had discovered were *Nicholas Nickleby*, *Oliver Twist*, *A Tale of Two Cities* and *Sketches by Boz*, and I devoured all of them quite greedily.

I had already read (and loved) *David Copperfield*, which I had found in the school library, so Dickens was no stranger to me. The *Sketches by Boz* were, of course, Dickens' early contributions to newspapers while he was a parliamentary reporter. Some of the pieces were investigative journalism; others were light essays and character sketches. Anyone wanting to take up journalism should read them; the young writer's enthusiasm comes through, and one realizes that journalism can be a noble profession and not necessarily a cynical one.

My favourite, though, was *Nickleby*, full of humour, pathos and memorable scenes.

I could identify with Nicholas in the same way that I could identify with David Copperfield; both sensitive young men trying to make their way in the literary or theatrical world, and encountering the most extraordinary characters along the way. On the other hand, I could not identify with young Oliver Twist, because I could not see him growing up; or the self-sacrificing Sydney Carton of *A Tale of Two Cities*: I couldn't see myself going to the guillotine to save my rival in love. No—off with *his* head!

I was in better company with Heathcliff, the obsessed, love-crazed monster of Emily Brontë's *Wuthering Heights*, which I had picked up along with the set of Dickens. It had been raining heavily all day, and by evening my room was leaking in several places. I set out mugs, basins and buckets in various spots, but I knew I would be awake all night all night unless the rain stopped.

The storm helped to create the right atmosphere, but even without it I would have been up all night, such was the hold that *Wuthering Heights* exerted over me. I read through the night, finishing the book only towards dawn, even as the wind and rain subsided and early morning light crept over the Sivalik hills.

That was nearly seventy years ago. Would this book cast the same spell on me today? One evening last month I came home with a copy in a new edition. And once again I was up all night, roaming those bleak Yorkshire moors, buffeted by the passions and anguish of those souls in torment. In her brief tenure on this earth, the most gifted of the three Brontë sisters, had put everything into this one sizzling novel and left it behind to haunt posterity. It is no

use giving the readers an extract. You have to take it in one
large dose, preferably late at night.

*

Talking of storms, no one could conjure up a storm at sea
more vividly than our ship's captain, Joseph Conrad, who
carried the manuscript of his first novel (*Almayer's Folly*)
about with him on his voyages for many years before
finding a publisher when he was nearing forty.

I never tire of reading *Typhoon*; I am carried along by
the rushing wind and tumbling waves; I become that little
steamer bobbing up and down in tremendous seas; I am
the captain, single-mindedly steering his ship against every
hostile element. Conrad's shorter works never cease to thrill
me—*The Shadow Line, Heart of Darkness, The End of the
Tether, An Outpost of Progress*. And this strange story, *The
Secret Sharer* (first published in *Harper's Magazine*, August–
September 1910), about a young captain on his first ship,
keyed up to win his crew's respect. But down in his cabin
hides another self, threatening his command, and yet in
the end, justifying it . . .

'The Secret Sharer' (1910)
by Joseph Conrad

I

On my right hand there were lines of fishing stakes resembling a mysterious system of half-submerged bamboo fences, incomprehensible in its division of the domain of tropical fishes, and crazy of aspect as if abandoned forever by some nomad tribe of fishermen now gone to the other end of the ocean; for there was no sign of human habitation as far as the eye could reach. To the left a group of barren islets, suggesting ruins of stone walls, towers, and blockhouses, had its foundations set in a blue sea that itself looked solid, so still and stable did it lie below my feet; even the track of light from the westering sun shone smoothly, without that animated glitter which tells of an imperceptible ripple. And when I turned my head to take a parting glance at the tug which had just left us anchored outside the bar, I saw the straight line of the flat shore joined to the stable sea, edge to edge, with a perfect and unmarked closeness, in one leveled floor half brown, half blue under the enormous dome of the sky. Corresponding in their insignificance to the islets of the sea, two small clumps of trees, one on each side of the only fault in the impeccable joint, marked the mouth of the river Meinam we had just left on the first preparatory stage of our homeward journey; and, far back on the inland level, a larger and loftier mass, the grove surrounding the great Paknam pagoda, was the only thing on which the eye could rest from the vain task of exploring the monotonous sweep of the horizon. Here and there gleams as of a few scattered pieces of silver marked the windings of the great river; and on the nearest of them, just within the bar, the tug steaming right into the land became lost to my sight, hull and funnel and masts, as though the impassive earth had swallowed her up without an effort, without a tremor. My eye followed the light cloud of her smoke, now here, now there, above the plain, according to the devious curves of the stream, but always fainter and farther away, till I lost it at last behind the miter-shaped hill of the great pagoda. And then I was left alone with my ship, anchored at the head of the Gulf of Siam.

She floated at the starting point of a long journey, very still in an immense stillness, the shadows of her spars flung far to the eastward by the setting sun. At that moment I was alone on her decks. There was not a sound in her—and around us nothing moved, nothing lived, not a canoe on the water, not a bird in the air, not a cloud in the sky. In this breathless pause at the threshold of a long passage we seemed to be measuring our fitness for a long and arduous enterprise, the appointed task of both our existences to be carried out, far from all human eyes, with only sky and sea for spectators and for judges.

There must have been some glare in the air to interfere with one's sight, because it was only just before the sun left us that my roaming eyes made out beyond the highest ridges of the principal islet of the group something which did away with the solemnity of perfect solitude. The tide of darkness flowed on swiftly; and with tropical suddenness a swarm of stars came out above the shadowy earth, while I lingered yet, my hand resting lightly on my ship's rail as if on the shoulder of a trusted friend. But, with all that multitude of celestial bodies staring down at one, the comfort of quiet communion with her was gone for good. And there were also disturbing sounds by this time— voices, footsteps forward; the steward flitted along the main-deck, a busily ministering spirit; a hand bell tinkled urgently under the poop deck . . .

I found my two officers waiting for me near the supper table, in the lighted cuddy. We sat down at once, and as I helped the chief mate, I said:

"Are you aware that there is a ship anchored inside the islands? I saw her mastheads above the ridge as the sun went down."

He raised sharply his simple face, overcharged by a terrible growth of whisker, and emitted his usual ejaculations: "Bless my soul, sir! You don't say so!"

My second mate was a round-cheeked, silent young man, grave beyond his years, I thought; but as our eyes happened to meet I detected a slight quiver on his lips. I looked down at once. It was not my part to encourage sneering on board my ship. It must be said, too, that I knew very little of my officers. In consequence of certain events of no particular significance, except to myself, I had been appointed to the command only a fortnight before. Neither did I know much of the hands forward. All these people had been together for eighteen months or so, and my position was that of the only stranger on board. I mention this because it has some bearing on what is to follow. But what I felt most was my being a stranger to the ship; and if all the truth must be told, I was somewhat of a stranger to myself. The youngest man on board (barring the second mate), and untried as yet by a position of the fullest responsibility, I was willing to take the adequacy of the others for granted. They had simply to be equal to their tasks; but I wondered how far I should turn out faithful to that ideal conception of one's own personality every man sets up for himself secretly.

Meantime the chief mate, with an almost visible effect of collaboration on the part of his round eyes and frightful whiskers, was trying to evolve a theory of the anchored ship. His dominant trait was to take all things into earnest consideration. He was of a painstaking turn of mind. As he used to say, he "liked to account to himself" for practically everything that came in his way, down to a miserable scorpion he had found in his cabin a week before. The why and the wherefore of that scorpion—how it got on board and came to select his room rather than the pantry (which was a dark place and more what a scorpion would be partial to), and how on earth it managed to drown itself in the inkwell of his writing desk—had exercised him infinitely. The ship within the islands was much more easily accounted for; and just as we were about to rise from table he made his pronouncement. She was, he doubted not, a ship from home lately arrived. Probably she drew too much water to cross the bar except at the top of spring tides. Therefore she went into that natural harbor to wait for a few days in preference to remaining in an open roadstead.

"That's so," confirmed the second mate, suddenly, in his slightly hoarse voice. "She draws over twenty feet. She's the Liverpool ship Sephora with a cargo of coal. Hundred and twenty-three days from Cardiff."

We looked at him in surprise.

"The tugboat skipper told me when he came on board for your letters, sir," explained the young man. "He expects to take her up the river the day after tomorrow."

After thus overwhelming us with the extent of his information he slipped out of the cabin. The mate observed regretfully that he "could not account for that young fellow's whims." What prevented him telling us all about it at once, he wanted to know.

I detained him as he was making a move. For the last two days the crew had had plenty of hard work, and the night before they had very little sleep. I felt painfully that I—a stranger—was doing something unusual when I directed him to let all hands turn in without setting an anchor watch. I proposed to keep on deck myself till one o'clock or thereabouts. I would get the second mate to relieve me at that hour.

"He will turn out the cook and the steward at four," I concluded, "and then give you a call. Of course at the slightest sign of any sort of wind we'll have the hands up and make a start at once."

He concealed his astonishment. "Very well, sir." Outside the cuddy he put his head in the second mate's door to inform him of my unheard-of caprice to take a five hours' anchor watch on myself. I heard the other raise his voice incredulously—"What? The Captain himself?" Then a few more murmurs, a door closed, then another. A few moments later I went on deck.

My strangeness, which had made me sleepless, had prompted that unconventional arrangement, as if I had expected in those solitary hours of the night to get on terms with the ship of which I knew nothing, manned by men of whom I knew very little more. Fast alongside a wharf, littered like any ship in port with a tangle of unrelated things, invaded by unrelated shore people, I had hardly seen her yet properly. Now, as she lay cleared for sea, the stretch of her main-deck seemed to me very fine under the stars. Very fine, very roomy for her size, and very inviting. I descended the poop and paced the waist, my mind picturing to myself the coming passage through the Malay Archipelago, down the Indian Ocean, and up the Atlantic. All its phases were familiar enough to me, every characteristic, all the alternatives which were likely to face me on the high seas—everything! . . . except the novel responsibility of command. But I took heart from the reasonable thought that the ship was like other ships, the men like other men, and that the sea was not likely to keep any special surprises expressly for my discomfiture.

Arrived at that comforting conclusion, I bethought myself of a cigar and went below to get it. All was still down there. Everybody at the after end of the ship was sleeping profoundly. I came out again on the quarter-deck, agreeably at ease in my sleeping suit on that warm breathless night, barefooted, a glowing cigar in my teeth, and, going forward, I was met by the profound silence of the fore end of the ship. Only as I passed the door of the forecastle, I heard a deep, quiet, trustful sigh of some sleeper inside. And suddenly I rejoiced in the great security of the sea as compared with the unrest of the land, in my choice of that untempted life presenting no disquieting problems, invested with an elementary moral beauty by the absolute straightforwardness of its appeal and by the singleness of its purpose.

The riding light in the forerigging burned with a clear, untroubled, as if symbolic, flame, confident and bright in the mysterious shades of the night. Passing on my way aft along the other side of the ship, I observed that the rope side ladder, put over, no doubt, for the master of the tug when he came to fetch away our letters, had not been hauled in as it should have been. I became annoyed at this, for exactitude in some small matters is the very soul of discipline. Then I reflected that I had myself peremptorily dismissed my officers from duty, and by my own act had prevented the anchor watch being formally set and things properly attended to. I asked myself whether it was wise ever to interfere with the established routine of duties even from the kindest of motives. My action might have made me appear eccentric. Goodness only knew how that absurdly whiskered mate would "account" for my conduct, and what the whole ship thought of that informality of their new captain. I was vexed with myself.

Not from compunction certainly, but, as it were mechanically, I proceeded to get the ladder in myself. Now a side ladder of that sort is a light affair and comes in easily, yet my vigorous tug, which should have brought it flying on board, merely recoiled upon my body in a totally unexpected jerk. What the devil! . . . I was so astounded by the immovableness of that ladder that I remained stock-still, trying to account for it to myself like that imbecile mate of mine. In the end, of course, I put my head over the rail.

The side of the ship made an opaque belt of shadow on the darkling glassy shimmer of the sea. But I saw at once something elongated and pale floating very close to the ladder. Before I could form a guess a faint flash of phosphorescent light, which seemed to issue suddenly from the naked body of a man, flickered in the sleeping water with the elusive, silent play of summer lightning in a night sky. With a gasp I saw revealed to my stare a pair of feet, the long legs, a broad livid back immersed right up to the neck in a greenish cadaverous glow. One hand, awash, clutched the bottom rung of the ladder. He was complete but for the head. A headless corpse! The cigar dropped out of my gaping mouth with a tiny plop and a short hiss quite audible in the absolute stillness of all things under heaven. At that I suppose he raised up his face, a dimly pale oval in the shadow of the ship's side. But even then I could only barely make out down there the shape of his black-haired head. However, it was enough for the horrid, frost-bound sensation which had gripped me about the chest to pass off. The moment of vain exclamations was past, too. I only climbed on the spare spar and leaned over the rail as far as I could, to bring my eyes nearer to that mystery floating alongside.

As he hung by the ladder, like a resting swimmer, the sea lightning played about his limbs at every stir; and he appeared in it ghastly, silvery, fishlike. He remained as mute as a fish, too. He made no motion to get out of the water, either. It was inconceivable that he should not attempt to come on board, and strangely troubling to suspect that perhaps he did not want to. And my first words were prompted by just that troubled incertitude.

"What's the matter?" I asked in my ordinary tone, speaking down to the face upturned exactly under mine.

"Cramp," it answered, no louder. Then slightly anxious, "I say, no need to call anyone."

"I was not going to," I said.

"Are you alone on deck?"

"Yes."

I had somehow the impression that he was on the point of letting go the ladder to swim away beyond my ken—mysterious as he came. But, for the moment, this being appearing as if he had risen from the bottom of the sea (it was certainly the nearest land to the ship) wanted only to know the time. I told him. And he, down there, tentatively:

"I suppose your captain's turned in?"

"I am sure he isn't," I said.

He seemed to struggle with himself, for I heard something like the low, bitter murmur of doubt. "What's the good?" His next words came out with a hesitating effort.

"Look here, my man. Could you call him out quietly?"

I thought the time had come to declare myself.

"I am the captain."

I heard a "By Jove!" whispered at the level of the water. The phosphorescence flashed in the swirl of the water all about his limbs, his other hand seized the ladder.

"My name's Leggatt."

The voice was calm and resolute. A good voice. The self-possession of that man had somehow induced a corresponding state in myself. It was very quietly that I remarked:

"You must be a good swimmer."

"Yes. I've been in the water practically since nine o'clock. The question for me now is whether I am to let go this ladder and go on swimming till I sink from exhaustion, or—to come on board here."

I felt this was no mere formula of desperate speech, but a real alternative in the view of a strong soul. I should have gathered from this that he was young; indeed, it is only the young who are ever confronted by such clear issues. But at the time it was pure intuition on my part. A mysterious communication was established already between us two—in the face of that silent, darkened tropical sea. I was young, too; young enough to make no comment. The man in the water began suddenly to climb up the ladder, and I hastened away from the rail to fetch some clothes.

Before entering the cabin I stood still, listening in the lobby at the foot of the stairs. A faint snore came through the closed door of the chief mate's room. The second mate's door was on the hook, but the darkness in there was absolutely soundless. He, too, was young and could sleep like a stone. Remained the steward, but he was not likely to wake up before he was called. I got a sleeping suit out of my room and, coming back on deck, saw the naked man from the sea sitting on the main hatch, glimmering white in the darkness, his elbows on his knees and his head in his hands. In a moment he had concealed his damp body in a sleeping suit of the same gray-stripe pattern as the one I was wearing and followed me like my double on the poop. Together we moved right aft, barefooted, silent.

"What is it?" I asked in a deadened voice, taking the lighted lamp out of the binnacle, and raising it to his face.

"An ugly business."

He had rather regular features; a good mouth; light eyes under somewhat heavy, dark eyebrows; a smooth, square forehead; no growth on his cheeks; a small, brown mustache, and a well-shaped, round chin. His expression was concentrated, meditative, under the inspecting light of the lamp I held up to his face; such as a man thinking hard in solitude might wear. My sleeping suit was just right for his size. A well-knit young fellow of twenty-five at most. He caught his lower lip with the edge of white, even teeth.

"Yes," I said, replacing the lamp in the binnacle. The warm, heavy tropical night closed upon his head again.

"There's a ship over there," he murmured.

"Yes, I know. The Sephora. Did you know of us?"

"Hadn't the slightest idea. I am the mate of her—" He paused and corrected himself. "I should say I *was*."

"Aha! Something wrong?"

"Yes. Very wrong indeed. I've killed a man."

"What do you mean? Just now?"

"No, on the passage. Weeks ago. Thirty-nine south. When I say a man—"

"Fit of temper," I suggested, confidently.

The shadowy, dark head, like mine, seemed to nod imperceptibly above the ghostly gray of my sleeping suit. It was, in the night, as though I had been faced by my own reflection in the depths of a somber and immense mirror.

"A pretty thing to have to own up to for a Conway boy," murmured my double, distinctly.

"You're a Conway boy?"

"I am," he said, as if startled. Then, slowly . . . "Perhaps you too—"

It was so; but being a couple of years older I had left before he joined. After a quick interchange of dates a silence fell; and I thought suddenly of my absurd mate with his terrific whiskers and the "Bless my soul—you don't say so" type of intellect. My double gave me an inkling of his thoughts by saying: "My father's a parson in Norfolk. Do you see me before a judge and jury on that charge? For myself I can't see the necessity. There are fellows that an angel from heaven—And I am not that. He was one of those creatures that are just simmering all the time with a silly sort of wickedness. Miserable devils that have no business to live at all. He wouldn't do his duty and wouldn't let anybody else do theirs. But what's the good of talking! You know well enough the sort of ill-conditioned snarling cur—"

He appealed to me as if our experiences had been as identical as our clothes. And I knew well enough the pestiferous danger of such a character where there are no means of legal repression. And I knew well enough also that my double there was no homicidal ruffian. I did not think of asking him for details, and he told me the story roughly in brusque, disconnected sentences. I needed no more. I saw it all going on as though I were myself inside that other sleeping suit.

"It happened while we were setting a reefed foresail, at dusk. Reefed foresail! You understand the sort of weather. The only sail we had left to keep the ship running; so you may guess what it had been like for days. Anxious sort of job, that. He gave me some of his cursed insolence at the sheet. I tell you I was overdone with this terrific weather that seemed to have no end to it. Terrific, I tell you—and a deep ship. I believe the fellow himself was half crazed with funk. It was no time for gentlemanly reproof, so I turned round and felled him like an ox. He up and at me. We closed just as an awful sea made for the ship. All hands saw it coming and took to the rigging, but I had him by the throat, and went on shaking him like a rat, the men above us yelling, 'Look out! look out!' Then a crash as if the sky had fallen on my head. They say that for over ten minutes hardly anything was to be seen of the ship—just the three masts and a bit of the forecastle head and of the poop all awash driving along in a smother of foam. It was a miracle that they found us, jammed together behind the forebitts. It's clear that I meant business, because I was holding him by the throat still when they picked us up. He was black in the face. It was too much for them. It seems they rushed us aft together, gripped as we were, screaming 'Murder!' like a lot of lunatics, and broke into the cuddy. And the ship running for her life, touch and go all the time, any minute her last in a sea fit to turn your hair gray only a-looking at it. I understand that the skipper, too, started raving like the rest of them. The man had been deprived of sleep for more than a week, and to have this sprung on him at the height of a furious gale nearly drove him out of his mind. I wonder they didn't fling me overboard after getting the carcass of their precious shipmate out of my fingers. They had rather a job to separate us, I've been told. A sufficiently fierce story to make an old judge and a respectable jury sit up a bit. The first thing I heard when I came to myself was the maddening howling of that endless gale, and on that the voice of the old man. He was hanging on to my bunk, staring into my face out of his sou'wester.

"'Mr. Leggatt, you have killed a man. You can act no longer as chief mate of this ship.'"

His care to subdue his voice made it sound monotonous. He rested a hand on the end of the skylight to steady himself with, and all that time did not stir a limb, so far as I could see. "Nice little tale for a quiet tea party," he concluded in the same tone.

One of my hands, too, rested on the end of the skylight; neither did I stir a limb, so far as I knew. We stood less than a foot from each other. It occurred to me that if old "Bless my soul—you don't say so" were to put his head up the companion and catch sight of us, he would think he was seeing double, or imagine himself come upon a scene of weird witchcraft; the strange captain having a quiet confabulation by the wheel with his own gray ghost. I became very much concerned to prevent anything of the sort. I heard the other's soothing undertone.

"My father's a parson in Norfolk," it said. Evidently he had forgotten he had told me this important fact before. Truly a nice little tale.

"You had better slip down into my stateroom now," I said, moving off stealthily. My double followed my movements; our bare feet made no sound; I let him in, closed the door with care, and, after giving a call to the second mate, returned on deck for my relief.

"Not much sign of any wind yet," I remarked when he approached.

"No, sir. Not much," he assented, sleepily, in his hoarse voice, with just enough deference, no more, and barely suppressing a yawn.

"Well, that's all you have to look out for. You have got your orders."

"Yes, sir."

I paced a turn or two on the poop and saw him take up his position face forward with his elbow in the ratlines of the mizzen rigging before I went below. The mate's faint snoring was still going on peacefully. The cuddy lamp was burning over the table on which stood a vase with flowers, a polite attention from the ship's provision merchant—the last flowers we should see for the next three months at the very least. Two bunches of bananas hung from the beam symmetrically, one on each side of the rudder casing. Everything was as before in the ship—except that two of her captain's sleeping suits were simultaneously in use, one motionless in the cuddy, the other keeping very still in the captain's stateroom.

It must be explained here that my cabin had the form of the capital letter L, the door being within the angle and opening into the short part of the letter. A couch was to the left, the bed place to the right; my writing desk and the chronometers' table faced the door. But anyone opening it, unless he stepped right inside, had no view of what I call the long (or vertical) part of the letter. It contained some lockers surmounted by a bookcase; and a few clothes, a thick jacket or two, caps, oilskin coat, and such like, hung on hooks. There was at the bottom of that part a door opening into my bathroom, which could be entered also directly from the saloon. But that way was never used.

The mysterious arrival had discovered the advantage of this particular shape. Entering my room, lighted strongly by a big bulkhead lamp swung on gimbals above my writing desk, I did not see him anywhere till he stepped out quietly from behind the coats hung in the recessed part.

"I heard somebody moving about, and went in there at once," he whispered.

I, too, spoke under my breath.

"Nobody is likely to come in here without knocking and getting permission."

He nodded. His face was thin and the sunburn faded, as though he had been ill. And no wonder. He had been, I heard presently, kept under arrest in his cabin for nearly seven weeks. But there was nothing sickly in his eyes or in his expression. He was not a bit like me, really; yet, as we stood leaning over my bed place, whispering side by side, with our dark heads together and our backs to the door, anybody bold enough to open it stealthily would have been treated to the uncanny sight of a double captain busy talking in whispers with his other self.

"But all this doesn't tell me how you came to hang on to our side ladder," I inquired, in the hardly audible murmurs we used, after he had told me something more of the proceedings on board the Sephora once the bad weather was over.

"When we sighted Java Head I had had time to think all those matters out several times over. I had six weeks of doing nothing else, and with only an hour or so every evening for a tramp on the quarter-deck."

He whispered, his arms folded on the side of my bed place, staring through the open port. And I could imagine perfectly the manner of this thinking out—a stubborn if not a steadfast operation; something of which I should have been perfectly incapable.

"I reckoned it would be dark before we closed with the land," he continued, so low that I had to strain my hearing near as we were to each other, shoulder touching shoulder almost. "So I asked to speak to the old man. He always seemed very sick when he came to see me—as if he could not look me in the face. You know, that foresail saved the ship. She was too deep to have run long under bare poles. And it was I that managed to set it for him. Anyway, he came. When I had him in my cabin—he stood by the door looking at me as if I had the halter round my neck already—I asked him right away to leave my cabin door unlocked at night while the ship was going through Sunda Straits. There would be the Java coast within two or three miles, off Angier Point. I wanted nothing more. I've had a prize for swimming my second year in the Conway."

"I can believe it," I breathed out.

"God only knows why they locked me in every night. To see some of their faces you'd have thought they were afraid I'd go about at night strangling people. Am I a murdering brute? Do I look it? By Jove! If I had been he wouldn't have trusted himself like that into my room. You'll say I might have chucked him aside and bolted out, there and then— it was dark already. Well, no. And for the same reason I wouldn't think of trying to smash the door. There would have been a rush to stop me at the noise, and I did not mean to get into a confounded scrimmage. Somebody else might have got killed—for I would not have broken out only to get chucked back, and I did not want any more of that work. He refused, looking more sick than ever. He was afraid of the men, and also of that old second mate of his who had been sailing with him for years—a gray-headed old humbug; and his steward, too, had been with him devil knows how long—seventeen years or more—a dogmatic sort of loafer who hated me like poison, just because I was the chief mate. No chief mate ever made more than one voyage in the Sephora, you know. Those two old chaps ran the ship. Devil only knows what the skipper wasn't afraid of (all his nerve went to pieces altogether in that hellish spell of bad weather we had)—of what the law would do to him—of his wife, perhaps. Oh, yes! she's on board. Though I don't think she would have meddled. She would have been only too glad to have me out of the ship in any way. The 'brand of Cain' business, don't you see. That's all right. I was ready enough to go off wandering on the face of the earth—and that was price enough to pay for an Abel of that sort. Anyhow, he wouldn't listen to me. 'This thing must take its course. I represent the law here.' He was shaking like a leaf. 'So you won't?' 'No!' 'Then I hope you will be able to sleep on that,' I said, and turned my back on him. 'I wonder that you can,' cries he, and locks the door.

"Well after that, I couldn't. Not very well. That was three weeks ago. We have had a slow passage through the Java Sea; drifted about Carimata for ten days. When we anchored here they thought, I suppose, it was all right. The nearest land (and that's five miles) is the ship's destination; the consul would soon set about catching me; and there would have been no object in holding to these islets there. I don't suppose there's a drop of water on them. I don't know how it was, but tonight that steward, after bringing me my supper, went out to let me eat it, and left the door unlocked. And I ate it—all there was, too. After I had finished I strolled out on the quarter-deck. I don't know that I meant to do anything. A breath of fresh air was all I wanted, I believe. Then a sudden temptation came over me. I kicked off my slippers and was in the water before I had made up my mind fairly. Somebody heard the splash and they raised an awful hullabaloo. 'He's gone! Lower the boats! He's committed suicide! No, he's swimming.' Certainly I was swimming. It's not so easy for a swimmer like me to commit suicide by drowning. I landed on the nearest islet before the boat left the ship's side. I heard them pulling about in the dark, hailing, and so on, but after a bit they gave up. Everything quieted down and the anchorage became still as death. I sat down on a stone and began to think. I felt certain they would start searching for me at daylight. There was no place to hide on those stony things—and if there had been, what would have been the good? But now I was clear of that ship, I was not going back. So after a while I took off all my clothes, tied them up in a bundle with a stone inside, and dropped them in the deep water on the outer side of that islet. That was suicide enough for me. Let them think what they liked, but I didn't mean to drown myself. I meant to swim till I sank—but that's not the same thing. I struck out for another of these little islands, and it was from that one that I first saw your riding light. Something to swim for. I went on easily, and on the way I came upon a flat rock a foot or two above water. In the daytime, I dare say, you might make it out with a glass from your poop. I scrambled up on it and rested myself for a bit. Then I made another start. That last spell must have been over a mile."

His whisper was getting fainter and fainter, and all the time he stared straight out through the porthole, in which there was not even a star to be seen. I had not interrupted him. There was something that made comment impossible in his narrative, or perhaps in himself; a sort of feeling, a quality, which I can't find a name for. And when he ceased, all I found was a futile whisper: "So you swam for our light?"

"Yes—straight for it. It was something to swim for. I couldn't see any stars low down because the coast was in the way, and I couldn't see the land, either. The water was like glass. One might have been swimming in a confounded thousand-feet deep cistern with no place for scrambling out anywhere; but what I didn't like was the notion of swimming round and round like a crazed bullock before I gave out; and as I didn't mean to go back . . . No. Do you see me being hauled back, stark naked, off one of these little islands by the scruff of the neck and fighting like a wild beast? Somebody would have got killed for certain, and I did not want any of that. So I went on. Then your ladder—"

"Why didn't you hail the ship?" I asked, a little louder.

He touched my shoulder lightly. Lazy footsteps came right over our heads and stopped. The second mate had crossed from the other side of the poop and might have been hanging over the rail for all we knew.

"He couldn't hear us talking—could he?" My double breathed into my very ear, anxiously.

His anxiety was in answer, a sufficient answer, to the question I had put to him. An answer containing all the difficulty of that situation. I closed the porthole quietly, to make sure. A louder word might have been overheard.

"Who's that?" he whispered then.

"My second mate. But I don't know much more of the fellow than you do."

And I told him a little about myself. I had been appointed to take charge while I least expected anything of the sort, not quite a fortnight ago. I didn't know either the ship or the people. Hadn't had the time in port to look about me or size anybody up. And as to the crew, all they knew was that I was appointed to take the ship home. For the rest, I was almost as much of a stranger on board as himself, I said. And at the moment I felt it most acutely. I felt that it would take very little to make me a suspect person in the eyes of the ship's company.

He had turned about meantime; and we, the two strangers in the ship, faced each other in identical attitudes.

"Your ladder—" he murmured, after a silence. "Who'd have thought of finding a ladder hanging over at night in a ship anchored out here! I felt just then a very unpleasant faintness. After the life I've been leading for nine weeks, anybody would have got out of condition. I wasn't capable of swimming round as far as your rudder chains. And, lo and behold! there was a ladder to get hold of. After I gripped it I said to myself, 'What's the good?' When I saw a man's head looking over I thought I would swim away presently and leave him shouting—in whatever language it was. I didn't mind being looked at. I—I liked it. And then you speaking to me so quietly—as if you had expected me—made me hold on a little longer. It had been a confounded lonely time—I don't mean while swimming. I was glad to talk a little to somebody that didn't belong to the Sephora. As to asking for the captain, that was a mere impulse. It could have been no use, with all the ship knowing about me and the other people pretty certain to be round here in the morning. I don't know—I wanted to be seen, to talk with somebody, before I went on. I don't know what I would have said . . . 'Fine night, isn't it?' or something of the sort."

"Do you think they will be round here presently?" I asked with some incredulity.

"Quite likely," he said, faintly.

"He looked extremely haggard all of a sudden. His head rolled on his shoulders.

"H'm. We shall see then. Meantime get into that bed," I whispered. "Want help? There."

It was a rather high bed place with a set of drawers underneath. This amazing swimmer really needed the lift I gave him by seizing his leg. He tumbled in, rolled over on his back, and flung one arm across his eyes. And then, with his face nearly hidden, he must have looked exactly as I used to look in that bed. I gazed upon my other self for a while before drawing across carefully the two green serge curtains which ran on a brass rod. I thought for a moment of pinning them together for greater safety, but I sat down on the couch, and once there I felt unwilling to rise and hunt for a pin. I would do it in a moment. I was extremely tired, in a peculiarly intimate way, by the strain of stealthiness, by the effort of whispering and the general secrecy of this excitement. It was three o'clock by now and I had been on my feet since nine, but I was not sleepy; I could not have gone to sleep. I sat there, fagged out, looking at the curtains, trying to clear my mind of the confused sensation of being in two places at once, and greatly bothered by an exasperating knocking in my head. It was a relief to discover suddenly that it was not in my head at all, but on the outside of the door. Before I could collect myself the words "Come in" were out of my mouth, and the steward entered with a tray, bringing in my morning coffee. I had slept, after all, and I was so frightened that I shouted, "This way! I am here, steward," as though he had been miles away. He put down the tray on the table next the couch and only then said, very quietly, "I can see you are here, sir." I felt him give me a keen look, but I dared not meet his eyes just then. He must have wondered why I had drawn the curtains of my bed before going to sleep on the couch. He went out, hooking the door open as usual.

I heard the crew washing decks above me. I knew I would have been told at once if there had been any wind. Calm, I thought, and I was doubly vexed. Indeed, I felt dual more than ever. The steward reappeared suddenly in the doorway. I jumped up from the couch so quickly that he gave a start.

"What do you want here?"

"Close your port, sir—they are washing decks."

"It is closed," I said, reddening.

"Very well, sir." But he did not move from the doorway and returned my stare in an extraordinary, equivocal manner for a time. Then his eyes wavered, all his expression changed, and in a voice unusually gentle, almost coaxingly:

"May I come in to take the empty cup away, sir?"

"Of course!" I turned my back on him while he popped in and out. Then I unhooked and closed the door and even pushed the bolt. This sort of thing could not go on very long. The cabin was as hot as an oven, too. I took a peep at my double, and discovered that he had not moved, his arm was still over his eyes; but his chest heaved; his hair was wet; his chin glistened with perspiration. I reached over him and opened the port.

"I must show myself on deck," I reflected.

Of course, theoretically, I could do what I liked, with no one to say nay to me within the whole circle of the horizon; but to lock my cabin door and take the key away I did not dare. Directly I put my head out of the companion I saw the group of my two officers, the second mate barefooted, the chief mate in long India-rubber boots, near the break of the poop, and the steward halfway down the poop ladder talking to them eagerly. He happened to catch sight of me and dived, the second ran down on the main-deck shouting some order or other, and the chief mate came to meet me, touching his cap.

There was a sort of curiosity in his eye that I did not like. I don't know whether the steward had told them that I was "queer" only, or downright drunk, but I know the man meant to have a good look at me. I watched him coming with a smile which, as he got into point-blank range, took effect and froze his very whiskers. I did not give him time to open his lips.

"Square the yards by lifts and braces before the hands go to breakfast."

It was the first particular order I had given on board that ship; and I stayed on deck to see it executed, too. I had felt the need of asserting myself without loss of time. That sneering young cub got taken down a peg or two on that occasion, and I also seized the opportunity of having a good look at the face of every foremast man as they filed past me to go to the after braces. At breakfast time, eating nothing myself, I presided with such frigid dignity that the two mates were only too glad to escape from the cabin as soon as decency permitted; and all the time the dual working of my mind distracted me almost to the point of insanity. I was constantly watching myself, my secret self, as dependent on my actions as my own personality, sleeping in that bed, behind that door which faced me as I sat at the head of the table. It was very much like being mad, only it was worse because one was aware of it.

I had to shake him for a solid minute, but when at last he opened his eyes it was in the full possession of his senses, with an inquiring look.

"All's well so far," I whispered. "Now you must vanish into the bathroom."

He did so, as noiseless as a ghost, and then I rang for the steward, and facing him boldly, directed him to tidy up my stateroom while I was having my bath—"and be quick about it." As my tone admitted of no excuses, he said, "Yes, sir," and ran off to fetch his dustpan and brushes. I took a bath and did most of my dressing, splashing, and whistling softly for the steward's edification, while the secret sharer of my life stood drawn up bolt upright in that little space, his face looking very sunken in daylight, his eyelids lowered under the stern, dark line of his eyebrows drawn together by a slight frown.

When I left him there to go back to my room the steward was finishing dusting. I sent for the mate and engaged him in some insignificant conversation. It was, as it were, trifling with the terrific character of his whiskers; but my object was to give him an opportunity for a good look at my cabin. And then I could at last shut, with a clear conscience, the door of my stateroom and get my double back into the recessed part. There was nothing else for it. He had to sit still on a small folding stool, half smothered by the heavy coats hanging there. We listened to the steward going into the bathroom out of the saloon, filling the water bottles there, scrubbing the bath, setting things to rights, whisk, bang, clatter—out again into the saloon—turn the key—click. Such was my scheme for keeping my second self invisible. Nothing better could be contrived under the circumstances. And there we sat; I at my writing desk ready to appear busy with some papers, he behind me out of sight of the door. It would not have been prudent to talk in daytime; and I could not have stood the excitement of that queer sense of whispering to myself. Now and then, glancing over my shoulder, I saw him far back there, sitting rigidly on the low stool, his bare feet close together, his arms folded, his head hanging on his breast—and perfectly still. Anybody would have taken him for me.

I was fascinated by it myself. Every moment I had to glance over my shoulder. I was looking at him when a voice outside the door said:

"Beg pardon, sir."

"Well! . . ." I kept my eyes on him, and so when the voice outside the door announced, "There's a ship's boat coming our way, sir," I saw him give a start—the first movement he had made for hours. But he did not raise his bowed head.

"All right. Get the ladder over."

I hesitated. Should I whisper something to him? But what? His immobility seemed to have been never disturbed. What could I tell him he did not know already? . . . Finally I went on deck.

II

The skipper of the Sephora had a thin red whisker all round his face, and the sort of complexion that goes with hair of that color; also the particular, rather smeary shade of blue in the eyes. He was not exactly a showy figure; his shoulders were high, his stature but middling—one leg slightly more bandy than the other. He shook hands, looking vaguely around. A spiritless tenacity was his main characteristic, I judged. I behaved with a politeness which seemed to disconcert him. Perhaps he was shy. He mumbled to me as if he were ashamed of what he was saying; gave his name (it was something like Archbold—but at this distance of years I hardly am sure), his ship's name, and a few other particulars of that sort, in the manner of a criminal making a reluctant and doleful confession. He had had terrible weather on the passage out—terrible—terrible—wife aboard, too.

By this time we were seated in the cabin and the steward brought in a tray with a bottle and glasses. "Thanks! No." Never took liquor. Would have some water, though. He drank two tumblerfuls. Terrible thirsty work. Ever since daylight had been exploring the islands round his ship.

"What was that for—fun?" I asked, with an appearance of polite interest.

"No!" He sighed. "Painful duty."

As he persisted in his mumbling and I wanted my double to hear every word, I hit upon the notion of informing him that I regretted to say I was hard of hearing.

"Such a young man, too!" he nodded, keeping his smeary blue, unintelligent eyes fastened upon me. "What was the cause of it—some disease?" he inquired, without the least sympathy and as if he thought that, if so, I'd got no more than I deserved.

"Yes; disease," I admitted in a cheerful tone which seemed to shock him. But my point was gained, because he had to raise his voice to give me his tale. It is not worthwhile to record his version. It was just over two months since all this had happened, and he had thought so much about it that he seemed completely muddled as to its bearings, but still immensely impressed.

"What would you think of such a thing happening on board your own ship? I've had the Sephora for these fifteen years. I am a well-known shipmaster."

He was densely distressed—and perhaps I should have sympathized with him if I had been able to detach my mental vision from the unsuspected sharer of my cabin as though he were my second self. There he was on the other side of the bulkhead, four or five feet from us, no more, as we sat in the saloon. I looked politely at Captain Archbold (if that was his name), but it was the other I saw, in a gray sleeping suit, seated on a low stool, his bare feet close together, his arms folded, and every word said between us falling into the ears of his dark head bowed on his chest.

"I have been at sea now, man and boy, for seven-and-thirty years, and I've never heard of such a thing happening in an English ship. And that it should be my ship. Wife on board, too."

I was hardly listening to him.

"Don't you think," I said, "that the heavy sea which, you told me, came aboard just then might have killed the man? I have seen the sheer weight of a sea kill a man very neatly, by simply breaking his neck."

"Good God!" he uttered, impressively, fixing his smeary blue eyes on me. "The sea! No man killed by the sea ever looked like that." He seemed positively scandalized at my suggestion. And as I gazed at him certainly not prepared for anything original on his part, he advanced his head close to mine and thrust his tongue out at me so suddenly that I couldn't help starting back.

After scoring over my calmness in this graphic way he nodded wisely. If I had seen the sight, he assured me, I would never forget it as long as I lived. The weather was too bad to give the corpse a proper sea burial. So next day at dawn they took it up on the poop, covering its face with a bit of bunting; he read a short prayer, and then, just as it was, in its oilskins and long boots, they launched it amongst those mountainous seas that seemed ready every moment to swallow up the ship herself and the terrified lives on board of her.

"That reefed foresail saved you," I threw in.

"Under God—it did," he exclaimed fervently. "It was by a special mercy, I firmly believe, that it stood some of those hurricane squalls."

"It was the setting of that sail which—" I began.

"God's own hand in it," he interrupted me. "Nothing less could have done it. I don't mind telling you that I hardly dared give the order. It seemed impossible that we could touch anything without losing it, and then our last hope would have been gone."

The terror of that gale was on him yet. I let him go on for a bit, then said, casually—as if returning to a minor subject:

"You were very anxious to give up your mate to the shore people, I believe?"

He was. To the law. His obscure tenacity on that point had in it something incomprehensible and a little awful; something, as it were, mystical, quite apart from his anxiety that he should not be suspected of "countenancing any doings of that sort." Seven-and-thirty virtuous years at sea, of which over twenty of immaculate command, and the last fifteen in the Sephora, seemed to have laid him under some pitiless obligation.

"And you know," he went on, groping shame-facedly amongst his feelings, "I did not engage that young fellow. His people had some interest with my owners. I was in a way forced to take him on. He looked very smart, very gentlemanly, and all that. But do you know—I never liked him, somehow. I am a plain man. You see, he wasn't exactly the sort for the chief mate of a ship like the Sephora."

I had become so connected in thoughts and impressions with the secret sharer of my cabin that I felt as if I, personally, were being given to understand that I, too, was not the sort that would have done for the chief mate of a ship like the Sephora. I had no doubt of it in my mind.

"Not at all the style of man. You understand," he insisted, superfluously, looking hard at me.

I smiled urbanely. He seemed at a loss for a while.

"I suppose I must report a suicide."

"Beg pardon?"

"Suicide! That's what I'll have to write to my owners directly I get in."

"Unless you manage to recover him before tomorrow," I assented, dispassionately . . . "I mean, alive."

He mumbled something which I really did not catch, and I turned my ear to him in a puzzled manner. He fairly bawled:

"The land—I say, the mainland is at least seven miles off my anchorage."

"About that."

My lack of excitement, of curiosity, of surprise, of any sort of pronounced interest, began to arouse his distrust. But except for the felicitous pretense of deafness I had not tried to pretend anything. I had felt utterly incapable of playing the part of ignorance properly, and therefore was afraid to try. It is also certain that he had brought some ready-made suspicions with him, and that he viewed my politeness as a strange and unnatural phenomenon. And yet how else could I have received him? Not heartily! That was impossible for psychological reasons, which I need not state here. My only object was to keep off his inquiries. Surlily? Yes, but surliness might have provoked a point-blank question. From its novelty to him and from its nature, punctilious courtesy was the manner best calculated to restrain the man. But there was the danger of his breaking through my defense bluntly. I could not, I think, have met him by a direct lie, also for psychological (not moral) reasons. If he had only known how afraid I was of his putting my feeling of identity with the other to the test! But, strangely enough—(I thought of it only afterwards)—I believe that he was not a little disconcerted by the reverse side of that weird situation, by something in me that reminded him of the man he was seeking—suggested a mysterious similitude to the young fellow he had distrusted and disliked from the first.

However that might have been, the silence was not very prolonged. He took another oblique step.

"I reckon I had no more than a two-mile pull to your ship. Not a bit more."

"And quite enough, too, in this awful heat," I said.

Another pause full of mistrust followed. Necessity, they say, is mother of invention, but fear, too, is not barren of ingenious suggestions. And I was afraid he would ask me point-blank for news of my other self.

"Nice little saloon, isn't it?" I remarked, as if noticing for the first time the way his eyes roamed from one closed door to the other. "And very well fitted out, too. Here, for instance," I continued, reaching over the back of my seat negligently and flinging the door open, "is my bathroom."

He made an eager movement, but hardly gave it a glance. I got up, shut the door of the bathroom, and invited him to have a look round, as if I were very proud of my accommodation. He had to rise and be shown round, but he went through the business without any raptures whatever.

"And now we'll have a look at my stateroom," I declared, in a voice as loud as I dared to make it, crossing the cabin to the starboard side with purposely heavy steps.

He followed me in and gazed around. My intelligent double had vanished. I played my part.

"Very convenient—isn't it?"

"Very nice. Very comf . . ." He didn't finish and went out brusquely as if to escape from some unrighteous wiles of mine. But it was not to be. I had been too frightened not to feel vengeful; I felt I had him on the run, and I meant to keep him on the run. My polite insistence must have had something menacing in it, because he gave in suddenly. And I did not let him off a single item; mate's room, pantry, storerooms, the very sail locker which was also under the poop—he had to look into them all. When at last I showed him out on the quarter-deck he drew a long, spiritless sigh, and mumbled dismally that he must really be going back to his ship now. I desired my mate, who had joined us, to see to the captain's boat.

The man of whiskers gave a blast on the whistle which he used to wear hanging round his neck, and yelled, "Sephora's away!" My double down there in my cabin must have heard, and certainly could not feel more relieved than I. Four fellows came running out from somewhere forward and went over the side, while my own men, appearing on deck too, lined the rail. I escorted my visitor to the gangway ceremoniously, and nearly overdid it. He was a tenacious beast. On the very ladder he lingered, and in that unique, guiltily conscientious manner of sticking to the point:

"I say . . . you . . . you don't think that—"

I covered his voice loudly:

"Certainly not . . . I am delighted. Good-by."

I had an idea of what he meant to say, and just saved myself by the privilege of defective hearing. He was too shaken generally to insist, but my mate, close witness of that parting, looked mystified and his face took on a thoughtful cast. As I did not want to appear as if I wished to avoid all communication with my officers, he had the opportunity to address me.

"Seems a very nice man. His boat's crew told our chaps a very extraordinary story, if what I am told by the steward is true. I suppose you had it from the captain, sir?"

"Yes. I had a story from the captain."

"A very horrible affair—isn't it, sir?"

"It is."

"Beats all these tales we hear about murders in Yankee ships."

"I don't think it beats them. I don't think it resembles them in the least."

"Bless my soul—you don't say so! But of course I've no acquaintance whatever with American ships, not I, so I couldn't go against your knowledge. It's horrible enough for me . . . But the queerest part is that those fellows seemed to have some idea the man was hidden aboard here. They had really. Did you ever hear of such a thing?"

"Preposterous—isn't it?"

We were walking to and fro athwart the quarter-deck. No one of the crew forward could be seen (the day was Sunday), and the mate pursued:

"There was some little dispute about it. Our chaps took offense. 'As if we would harbor a thing like that,' they said. 'Wouldn't you like to look for him in our coal-hole?' Quite a tiff. But they made it up in the end. I suppose he did drown himself. Don't you, sir?"

"I don't suppose anything."

"You have no doubt in the matter, sir?"

"None whatever."

I left him suddenly. I felt I was producing a bad impression, but with my double down there it was most trying to be on deck. And it was almost as trying to be below. Altogether a nerve-trying situation. But on the whole I felt less torn in two when I was with him. There was no one in the whole ship whom I dared take into my confidence. Since the hands had got to know his story, it would have been impossible to pass him off for anyone else, and an accidental discovery was to be dreaded now more than ever . . .

The steward being engaged in laying the table for dinner, we could talk only with our eyes when I first went down. Later in the afternoon we had a cautious try at whispering. The Sunday quietness of the ship was against us; the stillness of air and water around her was against us; the elements, the men were against us—everything was against us in our secret partnership; time itself—for this could not go on forever. The very trust in Providence was, I suppose, denied to his guilt. Shall I confess that this thought cast me down very much? And as to the chapter of accidents which counts for so much in the book of success, I could only hope that it was closed. For what favorable accident could be expected?

"Did you hear everything?" were my first words as soon as we took up our position side by side, leaning over my bed place.

He had. And the proof of it was his earnest whisper, "The man told you he hardly dared to give the order."

I understood the reference to be to that saving foresail.

"Yes. He was afraid of it being lost in the setting."

"I assure you he never gave the order. He may think he did, but he never gave it. He stood there with me on the break of the poop after the main topsail blew away, and whimpered about our last hope—positively whimpered about it and nothing else—and the night coming on! To hear one's skipper go on like that in such weather was enough to drive any fellow out of his mind. It worked me up into a sort of desperation. I just took it into my own hands and went away from him, boiling, and—But what's the use telling you? *You* know! . . . Do you think that if I had not been pretty fierce with them I should have got the men to do anything? Not I! The bo's'n perhaps? Perhaps! It wasn't a heavy sea—it was a sea gone mad! I suppose the end of the world will be something like that; and a man may have the heart to see it coming once and be done with it—but to have to face it day after day—I don't blame anybody. I was precious little better than the rest. Only—I was an officer of that old coal wagon, anyhow—"

"I quite understand," I conveyed that sincere assurance into his ear. He was out of breath with whispering; I could hear him pant slightly. It was all very simple. The same strung-up force which had given twenty-four men a chance, at least, for their lives, had, in a sort of recoil, crushed an unworthy mutinous existence.

But I had no leisure to weigh the merits of the matter—footsteps in the saloon, a heavy knock. "There's enough wind to get under way with, sir." Here was the call of a new claim upon my thoughts and even upon my feelings.

"Turn the hands up," I cried through the door. "I'll be on deck directly."

I was going out to make the acquaintance of my ship. Before I left the cabin our eyes met—the eyes of the only two strangers on board. I pointed to the recessed part where the little campstool awaited him and laid my finger on my lips. He made a gesture—somewhat vague—a little mysterious, accompanied by a faint smile, as if of regret.

This is not the place to enlarge upon the sensations of a man who feels for the first time a ship move under his feet to his own independent word. In my case they were not unalloyed. I was not wholly alone with my command; for there was that stranger in my cabin. Or rather, I was not completely and wholly with her. Part of me was absent. That mental feeling of being in two places at once affected me physically as if the mood of secrecy had penetrated my very soul. Before an hour had elapsed since the ship had begun to move, having occasion to ask the mate (he stood by my side) to take a compass bearing of the pagoda, I caught myself reaching up to his ear in whispers. I say I caught myself, but enough had escaped to startle the man. I can't describe it otherwise than by saying that he shied. A grave, preoccupied manner, as though he were in possession of some perplexing intelligence, did not leave him henceforth. A little later I moved away from the rail to look at the compass with such a stealthy gait that the helmsman noticed it—and I could not help noticing the unusual roundness of his eyes. These are trifling instances, though it's to no commander's advantage to be suspected of ludicrous eccentricities. But I was also more seriously affected. There are to a seaman certain words, gestures, that should in given conditions come as naturally, as instinctively as the winking of a menaced eye. A certain order should spring on to his lips without thinking; a certain sign should get itself made, so to speak, without reflection. But all unconscious alertness had abandoned me. I had to make an effort of will to recall myself back (from the cabin) to the conditions of the moment. I felt that I was appearing an irresolute commander to those people who were watching me more or less critically.

And, besides, there were the scares. On the second day out, for instance, coming off the deck in the afternoon (I had straw slippers on my bare feet) I stopped at the open pantry door and spoke to the steward. He was doing something there with his back to me. At the sound of my voice he nearly jumped out of his skin, as the saying is, and incidentally broke a cup.

"What on earth's the matter with you?" I asked, astonished.

He was extremely confused. "Beg your pardon, sir. I made sure you were in your cabin."

"You see I wasn't."

"No, sir. I could have sworn I had heard you moving in there not a moment ago. It's most extraordinary . . . very sorry, sir."

I passed on with an inward shudder. I was so identified with my secret double that I did not even mention the fact in those scanty, fearful whispers we exchanged. I suppose he had made some slight noise of some kind or other. It would have been miraculous if he hadn't at one time or another. And yet, haggard as he appeared, he looked always perfectly self-controlled, more than calm—almost invulnerable. On my suggestion he remained almost entirely in the bathroom, which, upon the whole, was the safest place. There could be really no shadow of an excuse for anyone ever wanting to go in there, once the steward had done with it. It was a very tiny place. Sometimes he reclined on the floor, his legs bent, his head sustained on one elbow. At others I would find him on the campstool, sitting in his gray sleeping suit and with his cropped dark hair like a patient, unmoved convict. At night I would smuggle him into my bed place, and we would whisper together, with the regular footfalls of the officer of the watch passing and repassing over our heads. It was an infinitely miserable time. It was lucky that some tins of fine preserves were stowed in a locker in my stateroom; hard bread I could always get hold of; and so he lived on stewed chicken, *Pate de Foie Gras*, asparagus, cooked oysters, sardines—on all sorts of abominable sham delicacies out of tins. My early-morning coffee he always drank; and it was all I dared do for him in that respect.

Every day there was the horrible maneuvering to go through so that my room and then the bathroom should be done in the usual way. I came to hate the sight of the steward, to abhor the voice of that harmless man. I felt that it was he who would bring on the disaster of discovery. It hung like a sword over our heads.

The fourth day out, I think (we were then working down the east side of the Gulf of Siam, tack for tack, in light winds and smooth water)—the fourth day, I say, of this miserable juggling with the unavoidable, as we sat at our evening meal, that man, whose slightest movement I dreaded, after putting down the dishes ran up on deck busily. This could not be dangerous. Presently he came down again; and then it appeared that he had remembered a coat of mine which I had thrown over a rail to dry after having been wetted in a shower which had passed over the ship in the afternoon. Sitting stolidly at the head of the table I became terrified at the sight of the garment on his arm. Of course he made for my door. There was no time to lose.

"Steward," I thundered. My nerves were so shaken that I could not govern my voice and conceal my agitation. This was the sort of thing that made my terrifically whiskered mate tap his forehead with his forefinger. I had detected him using that gesture while talking on deck with a confidential air to the carpenter. It was too far to hear a word, but I had no doubt that this pantomime could only refer to the strange new captain.

"Yes, sir," the pale-faced steward turned resignedly to me. It was this maddening course of being shouted at, checked without rhyme or reason, arbitrarily chased out of my cabin, suddenly called into it, sent flying out of his pantry on incomprehensible errands, that accounted for the growing wretchedness of his expression.

"Where are you going with that coat?"

"To your room, sir."

"Is there another shower coming?"

"I'm sure I don't know, sir. Shall I go up again and see, sir?"

"No! never mind."

My object was attained, as of course my other self in there would have heard everything that passed. During this interlude my two officers never raised their eyes off their respective plates; but the lip of that confounded cub, the second mate, quivered visibly.

I expected the steward to hook my coat on and come out at once. He was very slow about it; but I dominated my nervousness sufficiently not to shout after him. Suddenly I became aware (it could be heard plainly enough) that the fellow for some reason or other was opening the door of the bathroom. It was the end. The place was literally not big enough to swing a cat in. My voice died in my throat and I went stony all over. I expected to hear a yell of surprise and terror, and made a movement, but had not the strength to get on my legs. Everything remained still. Had my second self taken the poor wretch by the throat? I don't know what I could have done next moment if I had not seen the steward come out of my room, close the door, and then stand quietly by the sideboard.

"Saved," I thought. "But, no! Lost! Gone! He was gone!"

I laid my knife and fork down and leaned back in my chair. My head swam. After a while, when sufficiently recovered to speak in a steady voice, I instructed my mate to put the ship round at eight o'clock himself.

"I won't come on deck," I went on. "I think I'll turn in, and unless the wind shifts I don't want to be disturbed before midnight. I feel a bit seedy."

"You did look middling bad a little while ago," the chief mate remarked without showing any great concern.

They both went out, and I stared at the steward clearing the table. There was nothing to be read on that wretched man's face. But why did he avoid my eyes, I asked myself. Then I thought I should like to hear the sound of his voice.

"Steward!"

"Sir!" Startled as usual.

"Where did you hang up that coat?"

"In the bathroom, sir." The usual anxious tone. "It's not quite dry yet, sir."

For some time longer I sat in the cuddy. Had my double vanished as he had come? But of his coming there was an explanation, whereas his disappearance would be inexplicable . . . I went slowly into my dark room, shut the door, lighted the lamp, and for a time dared not turn round. When at last I did I saw him standing bolt-upright in the narrow recessed part. It would not be true to say I had a shock, but an irresistible doubt of his bodily existence flitted through my mind. Can it be, I asked myself, that he is not visible to other eyes than mine? It was like being haunted. Motionless, with a grave face, he raised his hands slightly at me in a gesture which meant clearly, "Heavens! what a narrow escape!" Narrow indeed. I think I had come creeping quietly as near insanity as any man who has not actually gone over the border. That gesture restrained me, so to speak.

The mate with the terrific whiskers was now putting the ship on the other tack. In the moment of profound silence which follows upon the hands going to their stations I heard on the poop his raised voice: "Hard alee!" and the distant shout of the order repeated on the main-deck. The sails, in that light breeze, made but a faint fluttering noise. It ceased. The ship was coming round slowly: I held my breath in the renewed stillness of expectation; one wouldn't have thought that there was a single living soul on her decks. A sudden brisk shout, "Mainsail haul!" broke the spell, and in the noisy cries and rush overhead of the men running away with the main brace we two, down in my cabin, came together in our usual position by the bed place.

He did not wait for my question. "I heard him fumbling here and just managed to squat myself down in the bath," he whispered to me. "The fellow only opened the door and put his arm in to hang the coat up. All the same—"

"I never thought of that," I whispered back, even more appalled than before at the closeness of the shave, and marveling at that something unyielding in his character which was carrying him through so finely. There was no agitation in his whisper. Whoever was being driven distracted, it was not he. He was sane. And the proof of his sanity was continued when he took up the whispering again.

"It would never do for me to come to life again."

It was something that a ghost might have said. But what he was alluding to was his old captain's reluctant admission of the theory of suicide. It would obviously serve his turn—if I had understood at all the view which seemed to govern the unalterable purpose of his action.

"You must maroon me as soon as ever you can get amongst these islands off the Cambodge shore," he went on.

"Maroon you! We are not living in a boy's adventure tale," I protested. His scornful whispering took me up.

"We aren't indeed! There's nothing of a boy's tale in this. But there's nothing else for it. I want no more. You don't suppose I am afraid of what can be done to me? Prison or gallows or whatever they may please. But you don't see me coming back to explain such things to an old fellow in a wig and twelve respectable tradesmen, do you? What can they know whether I am guilty or not—or of *what* I am guilty, either? That's my affair. What does the Bible say? 'Driven off the face of the earth.' Very well, I am off the face of the earth now. As I came at night so I shall go."

"Impossible!" I murmured. "You can't."

"Can't? . . . Not naked like a soul on the Day of Judgment. I shall freeze on to this sleeping suit. The Last Day is not yet—and . . . you have understood thoroughly. Didn't you?"

I felt suddenly ashamed of myself. I may say truly that I understood—and my hesitation in letting that man swim away from my ship's side had been a mere sham sentiment, a sort of cowardice.

"It can't be done now till next night," I breathed out. "The ship is on the off-shore tack and the wind may fail us."

"As long as I know that you understand," he whispered. "But of course you do. It's a great satisfaction to have got somebody to understand. You seem to have been there on purpose." And in the same whisper, as if we two whenever we talked had to say things to each other which were not fit for the world to hear, he added, "It's very wonderful."

We remained side by side talking in our secret way but sometimes silent or just exchanging a whispered word or two at long intervals. And as usual he stared through the port. A breath of wind came now and again into our faces. The ship might have been moored in dock, so gently and on an even keel she slipped through the water, that did not murmur even at our passage, shadowy and silent like a phantom sea.

At midnight I went on deck, and to my mate's great surprise put the ship round on the other tack. His terrible whiskers flitted round me in silent criticism. I certainly should not have done it if it had been only a question of getting out of that sleepy gulf as quickly as possible. I believe he told the second mate, who relieved him, that it was a great want of judgment. The other only yawned. That intolerable cub shuffled about so sleepily and lolled against the rails in such a slack, improper fashion that I came down on him sharply.

"Aren't you properly awake yet?"

"Yes, sir! I am awake."

"Well, then, be good enough to hold yourself as if you were. And keep a lookout. If there's any current we'll be closing with some islands before daylight."

The east side of the gulf is fringed with islands, some solitary, others in groups. On the blue background of the high coast they seem to float on silvery patches of calm water, arid and gray, or dark green and rounded like clumps of evergreen bushes, with the larger ones, a mile or two long, showing the outlines of ridges, ribs of gray rock under the dark mantle of matted leafage. Unknown to trade, to travel, almost to geography, the manner of life they harbor is an unsolved secret. There must be villages—settlements of fishermen at least—on the largest of them, and some communication with the world is probably kept up by native craft. But all that forenoon, as we headed for them, fanned along by the faintest of breezes, I saw no sign of man or canoe in the field of the telescope I kept on pointing at the scattered group.

At noon I gave no orders for a change of course, and the mate's whiskers became much concerned and seemed to be offering themselves unduly to my notice. At last I said:

"I am going to stand right in. Quite in—as far as I can take her."

The stare of extreme surprise imparted an air of ferocity also to his eyes, and he looked truly terrific for a moment.

"We're not doing well in the middle of the gulf," I continued, casually. "I am going to look for the land breezes tonight."

"Bless my soul! Do you mean, sir, in the dark amongst the lot of all them islands and reefs and shoals?"

"Well—if there are any regular land breezes at all on this coast one must get close inshore to find them, mustn't one?"

"Bless my soul!" he exclaimed again under his breath. All that afternoon he wore a dreamy, contemplative appearance which in him was a mark of perplexity. After dinner I went into my stateroom as if I meant to take some rest. There we two bent our dark heads over a half-unrolled chart lying on my bed.

"There," I said. "It's got to be Koh-ring. I've been looking at it ever since sunrise. It has got two hills and a low point. It must be inhabited. And on the coast opposite there is what looks like the mouth of a biggish river—with some towns, no doubt, not far up. It's the best chance for you that I can see."

"Anything. Koh-ring let it be."

He looked thoughtfully at the chart as if surveying chances and distances from a lofty height—and following with his eyes his own figure wandering on the blank land of Cochin-China, and then passing off that piece of paper clean out of sight into uncharted regions. And it was as if the ship had two captains to plan her course for her. I had been so worried and restless running up and down that I had not had the patience to dress that day. I had remained in my sleeping suit, with straw slippers and a soft floppy hat. The closeness of the heat in the gulf had been most oppressive, and the crew were used to seeing me wandering in that airy attire.

"She will clear the south point as she heads now," I whispered into his ear. "Goodness only knows when, though, but certainly after dark. I'll edge her in to half a mile, as far as I may be able to judge in the dark—"

"Be careful," he murmured, warningly—and I realized suddenly that all my future, the only future for which I was fit, would perhaps go irretrievably to pieces in any mishap to my first command.

I could not stop a moment longer in the room. I motioned him to get out of sight and made my way on the poop. That unplayful cub had the watch. I walked up and down for a while thinking things out, then beckoned him over.

"Send a couple of hands to open the two quarter-deck ports," I said, mildly.

He actually had the impudence, or else so forgot himself in his wonder at such an incomprehensible order, as to repeat:

"Open the quarter-deck ports! What for, sir?"

"The only reason you need concern yourself about is because I tell you to do so. Have them open wide and fastened properly."

He reddened and went off, but I believe made some jeering remark to the carpenter as to the sensible practice of ventilating a ship's quarter-deck. I know he popped into the mate's cabin to impart the fact to him because the whiskers came on deck, as it were by chance, and stole glances at me from below—for signs of lunacy or drunkenness, I suppose.

A little before supper, feeling more restless than ever, I rejoined, for a moment, my second self. And to find him sitting so quietly was surprising, like something against nature, inhuman.

I developed my plan in a hurried whisper.

"I shall stand in as close as I dare and then put her round. I will presently find means to smuggle you out of here into the sail locker, which communicates with the lobby. But there is an opening, a sort of square for hauling the sails out, which gives straight on the quarter-deck and which is never closed in fine weather, so as to give air to the sails. When the ship's way is deadened in stays and all the hands are aft at the main braces you will have a clear road to slip out and get overboard through the open quarter-deck port. I've had them both fastened up. Use a rope's end to lower yourself into the water so as to avoid a splash—you know. It could be heard and cause some beastly complication."

He kept silent for a while, then whispered, "I understand."

"I won't be there to see you go," I began with an effort. "The rest . . . I only hope I have understood, too."

"You have. From first to last"—and for the first time there seemed to be a faltering, something strained in his whisper. He caught hold of my arm, but the ringing of the supper bell made me start. He didn't though; he only released his grip.

After supper I didn't come below again till well past eight o'clock. The faint, steady breeze was loaded with dew; and the wet, darkened sails held all there was of propelling power in it. The night, clear and starry, sparkled darkly, and the opaque, lightless patches shifting slowly against the low stars were the drifting islets. On the port bow there was a big one more distant and shadowily imposing by the great space of sky it eclipsed.

On opening the door I had a back view of my very own self looking at a chart. He had come out of the recess and was standing near the table.

"Quite dark enough," I whispered.

He stepped back and leaned against my bed with a level, quiet glance. I sat on the couch. We had nothing to say to each other. Over our heads the officer of the watch moved here and there. Then I heard him move quickly. I knew what that meant. He was making for the companion; and presently his voice was outside my door.

"We are drawing in pretty fast, sir. Land looks rather close."

"Very well," I answered. "I am coming on deck directly."

I waited till he was gone out of the cuddy, then rose. My double moved too. The time had come to exchange our last whispers, for neither of us was ever to hear each other's natural voice.

"Look here!" I opened a drawer and took out three sovereigns. "Take this anyhow. I've got six and I'd give you the lot, only I must keep a little money to buy some fruit and vegetables for the crew from native boats as we go through Sunda Straits."

He shook his head.

"Take it," I urged him, whispering desperately. "No one can tell what—"

He smiled and slapped meaningly the only pocket of the sleeping jacket. It was not safe, certainly. But I produced a large old silk handkerchief of mine, and tying the three pieces of gold in a corner, pressed it on him. He was touched, I supposed, because he took it at last and tied it quickly round his waist under the jacket, on his bare skin.

Our eyes met; several seconds elapsed, till, our glances still mingled, I extended my hand and turned the lamp out. Then I passed through the cuddy, leaving the door of my room wide open . . . "Steward!"

He was still lingering in the pantry in the greatness of his zeal, giving a rub-up to a plated cruet stand the last thing before going to bed. Being careful not to wake up the mate, whose room was opposite, I spoke in an undertone.

He looked round anxiously. "Sir!"

"Can you get me a little hot water from the galley?"

"I am afraid, sir, the galley fire's been out for some time now."

"Go and see."

He flew up the stairs.

"Now," I whispered, loudly, into the saloon—too loudly, perhaps, but I was afraid I couldn't make a sound. He was by my side in an instant—the double captain slipped past the stairs—through a tiny dark passage . . . a sliding door. We were in the sail locker, scrambling on our knees over the sails. A sudden thought struck me. I saw myself wandering barefooted, bareheaded, the sun beating on my dark poll. I snatched off my floppy hat and tried hurriedly in the dark to ram it on my other self. He dodged and fended off silently. I wonder what he thought had come to me before he understood and suddenly desisted. Our hands met gropingly, lingered united in a steady, motionless clasp for a second . . . No word was breathed by either of us when they separated.

I was standing quietly by the pantry door when the steward returned.

"Sorry, sir. Kettle barely warm. Shall I light the spirit lamp?"

"Never mind."

I came out on deck slowly. It was now a matter of conscience to shave the land as close as possible—for now he must go overboard whenever the ship was put in stays. Must! There could be no going back for him. After a moment I walked over to leeward and my heart flew into my mouth at the nearness of the land on the bow. Under any other circumstances I would not have held on a minute longer. The second mate had followed me anxiously.

I looked on till I felt I could command my voice.

"She will weather," I said then in a quiet tone.

"Are you going to try that, sir?" he stammered out incredulously.

I took no notice of him and raised my tone just enough to be heard by the helmsman.

"Keep her good full."

"Good full, sir."

The wind fanned my cheek, the sails slept, the world was silent. The strain of watching the dark loom of the land grow bigger and denser was too much for me. I had shut my eyes—because the ship must go closer. She must! The stillness was intolerable. Were we standing still?

When I opened my eyes the second view started my heart with a thump. The black southern hill of Koh-ring seemed to hang right over the ship like a towering fragment of everlasting night. On that enormous mass of blackness there was not a gleam to be seen, not a sound to be heard. It was gliding irresistibly towards us and yet seemed already within reach of the hand. I saw the vague figures of the watch grouped in the waist, gazing in awed silence.

"Are you going on, sir?" inquired an unsteady voice at my elbow.

I ignored it. I had to go on.

"Keep her full. Don't check her way. That won't do now," I said warningly.

"I can't see the sails very well," the helmsman answered me, in strange, quavering tones.

Was she close enough? Already she was, I won't say in the shadow of the land, but in the very blackness of it, already swallowed up as it were, gone too close to be recalled, gone from me altogether.

"Give the mate a call," I said to the young man who stood at my elbow as still as death. "And turn all hands up."

My tone had a borrowed loudness reverberated from the height of the land. Several voices cried out together: "We are all on deck, sir."

Then stillness again, with the great shadow gliding closer, towering higher, without a light, without a sound. Such a hush had fallen on the ship that she might have been a bark of the dead floating in slowly under the very gate of Erebus.

"My God! Where are we?"

It was the mate moaning at my elbow. He was thunderstruck, and as it were deprived of the moral support of his whiskers. He clapped his hands and absolutely cried out, "Lost!"

"Be quiet," I said, sternly.

He lowered his tone, but I saw the shadowy gesture of his despair. "What are we doing here?"

"Looking for the land wind."

He made as if to tear his hair, and addressed me recklessly.

"She will never get out. You have done it, sir. I knew it'd end in something like this. She will never weather, and you are too close now to stay. She'll drift ashore before she's round. Oh my God!"

I caught his arm as he was raising it to batter his poor devoted head, and shook it violently.

"She's ashore already," he wailed, trying to tear himself away.

"Is she? . . . Keep good full there!"

"Good full, sir," cried the helmsman in a frightened, thin, childlike voice.

I hadn't let go the mate's arm and went on shaking it. "Ready about, do you hear? You go forward"—shake—"and stop there"—shake—"and hold your noise"—shake—"and see these head-sheets properly overhauled"—shake, shake—shake.

And all the time I dared not look towards the land lest my heart should fail me. I released my grip at last and he ran forward as if fleeing for dear life.

I wondered what my double there in the sail locker thought of this commotion. He was able to hear everything—and perhaps he was able to understand why, on my conscience, it had to be thus close—no less. My first order "Hard alee!" re-echoed ominously under the towering shadow of Koh-ring as if I had shouted in a mountain gorge. And then I watched the land intently. In that smooth water and light wind it was impossible to feel the ship coming-to. No! I could not feel her. And my second self was making now ready to ship out and lower himself overboard. Perhaps he was gone already . . .?

The great black mass brooding over our very mastheads began to pivot away from the ship's side silently. And now I forgot the secret stranger ready to depart, and remembered only that I was a total stranger to the ship. I did not know her. Would she do it? How was she to be handled?

I swung the mainyard and waited helplessly. She was perhaps stopped, and her very fate hung in the balance, with the black mass of Koh-ring like the gate of the everlasting night towering over her taffrail. What would she do now? Had she way on her yet? I stepped to the side swiftly, and on the shadowy water I could see nothing except a faint phosphorescent flash revealing the glassy smoothness of the sleeping surface. It was impossible to tell—and I had not learned yet the feel of my ship. Was she moving? What I needed was something easily seen, a piece of paper, which I could throw overboard and watch. I had nothing on me. To run down for it I didn't dare. There was no time. All at once my strained, yearning stare distinguished a white object floating within a yard of the ship's side. White on the black water. A phosphorescent flash passed under it. What was that thing? . . . I recognized my own floppy hat. It must have fallen off his head . . . and he didn't bother. Now I had what I wanted—the saving mark for my eyes. But I hardly thought of my other self, now gone from the ship, to be hidden forever from all friendly faces, to be a fugitive and a vagabond on the earth, with no brand of the curse on his sane forehead to stay a slaying hand . . . too proud to explain.

And I watched the hat—the expression of my sudden pity for his mere flesh. It had been meant to save his homeless head from the dangers of the sun. And now—behold—it was saving the ship, by serving me for a mark to help out the ignorance of my strangeness. Ha! It was drifting forward, warning me just in time that the ship had gathered sternaway.

"Shift the helm," I said in a low voice to the seaman standing still like a statue.

The man's eyes glistened wildly in the binnacle light as he jumped round to the other side and spun round the wheel.

I walked to the break of the poop. On the over-shadowed deck all hands stood by the forebraces waiting for my order. The stars ahead seemed to be gliding from right to left. And all was so still in the world that I heard the quiet remark, "She's round," passed in a tone of intense relief between two seamen.

"Let go and haul."

The foreyards ran round with a great noise, amidst cheery cries. And now the frightful whiskers made themselves heard giving various orders. Already the ship was drawing ahead. And I was alone with her. Nothing! no one in the world should stand now between us, throwing a shadow on the way of silent knowledge and mute affection, the perfect communion of a seaman with his first command.

Walking to the taffrail, I was in time to make out, on the very edge of a darkness thrown by a towering black mass like the very gateway of Erebus—yes, I was in time to catch an evanescent glimpse of my white hat left behind to mark the spot where the secret sharer of my cabin and of my thoughts, as though he were my second self, had lowered himself into the water to take his punishment: a free man, a proud swimmer striking out for a new destiny.

9

Making My Own Bed

Whenever a young person asks me for some really serious advice, I say, 'Always make your own bed.' And, invariably, my young friend goes away laughing, saying, 'Bond Uncle is never serious about anything.'

But I am dead serious. Making one's own bed is a stamp of personality, a statement about being someone different upon this earth, a unique expression of one's individuality. Don't leave it to your mother or sister or the domestic help; it will become their kind of bed, and you will have to fit your personality to suit theirs.

Apart from that, it can be a matter of self-preservation.

Not so long ago I was put up in a guest house on the edge of the desert in Jodhpur, Rajasthan. At night I retired to my room. The bed was neatly made. Too neat for my liking. I lifted the pillow and discovered an enormous black scorpion welcoming me with sting upraised. Well, I am not one to kill any of God's creatures without good reason, and so, using a pencil (they have their uses), I tipped the scorpion into a large plastic mug, opened a window, and deposited the visitor into a flower bed.

Returning to the bed, I decided a little rearrangement of the mattresses was in order. On lifting one up, I discovered an entire nest of scorpions. Disturbed by my interference, scores of young scorpions were soon scampering about on the bed sheets. I made a tactical retreat. The railway station was not far away, and I spent the night in an armchair in the station waiting room. Better a railway bug than a desert scorpion!

*

Making my own bed was something I learnt to do during my school days when, as a boarder, we were at the mercy of prefects, housemasters and occasional pranksters. We made our own bed, polished our own shoes, and washed behind the ears with Lifebuoy soap. Occasionally a bright spark would introduce some stinging nettle between our sheets, and we would retaliate in kind, preferably with a spiky cactus. 'French' beds were popular—the sheets were arranged in such a way that the occupant, getting between them, found himself in an inextricable tangle.

All this meant that we had to be very protective of our beds. Not only did we make our own beds but we also had to guard against all kinds of interlopers.

I became so protective of my bed that when I went to London as a young man and rented a bed–sitting room from a motherly Jewish landlady, I had a regular tussle with her over who had the right to make my bed. She insisted that as I was her boarder, with a right to sharing the bathroom, she had a right to tidying my bedroom, including the bed. I would make the bed. She would remake it. I would make it again. Sometimes she won; sometimes I did. In the end we compromised. She would make the bed in the morning, so that I wouldn't be late for work. And in the evenings, when I returned, I could make it again!

When winter came, this kind lady produced an old-fashioned stone hot water bottle, which was most effective. It kept my feet warm all night. As a result I surrendered all bed-making rights to her. A warm bed and a good breakfast, what more can a young man ask for?

*

Good breakfasts can be had in many of our starred hotels, but I have never really been happy with the beds. For a start, there are far too many pillows. These are flung away before I lie down. How can one sleep propped up like the desiccated corpse in *Psycho*? Then the sheets and blankets have to be loosened, as these are always wedged under the mattress too tightly. Then the mattresses are often too springy and propel you towards the ceiling if you flop on to them suddenly. I have sometimes found it easier to sleep on the floor, using a pillow and blanket from the bed and a thick rug beneath me.

Hotel rooms are very similar to each other, so don't forget your room number. On one occasion I stepped out of my room, leaving the door slightly ajar, to see if there was a stairway at the end of the corridor. (I'm paranoid about lifts and avoid them if I can.) On returning to the room, the door being open, I found the bed occupied by a large lady in a pink nightdress. I was in the wrong room. Fortunately, the lady did not scream, and I backed out, apologizing profusely. She seemed to recognize me, even though she got my name wrong.

'Aren't you that writer fellow, Bunskin Rond?' she asked in good humour. 'Come on in and have a martini.'

Fond as I am of a martini, I thought it wise to beat a hasty retreat.

Stick to your own bedroom, Bunskin.

*

A writer who often found himself in the wrong bedroom was Laurence Sterne, the author of *Tristram Shandy*. This witty, irreverent clergyman spent more time flirting with chambermaids than he did in composing sermons. In his writing he broke all the rules of grammar and punctuation, ignoring the demands of plot, time sequences, etc. and hopping like a grasshopper from one unrelated incident to another. Only a genius such as Sterne could get away with it.

In *A Sentimental Journey Through France and Italy* (1768) he careers about the Continent, staying in various inns and hotels, and losing no time in striking up a rapport with chambermaids or ladies of fashion. In this delightful sequence he is forced to share a room with a lady and her maid. He does so with elan; unlike poor Mr. Pickwick (in *Pickwick Papers*) who wanders into the wrong bedroom and gets into trouble.

One could compile an anthology of stories about travellers finding themselves in strange beds or bedrooms, starting with Thackeray's *A Terribly Strange Bed*. I have started collecting for such a book. Meanwhile, enjoy this delightful chapter from the work of our mischievous and freewheeling clergyman.

From *A Sentimental Journey Through*
France & Italy (1768)
by Laurence Sterne

The Case of Delicacy

When you have gained the top of mount Taurira, you run presently down to Lyons—adieu then to all rapid movements! 'Tis a journey of caution; and it fares better with sentiments, not to be in a hurry with them; so I contracted with a voiturin to take his time with a couple of mules, and convey me in my own chaise safe to Turin through Savoy.

Poor, patient, quiet, honest people! fear not; your poverty, the treasury of your simple virtues, will not be envied you by the world, nor will your vallies be invaded by it.—Nature! in the midst of thy disorders, thou art still friendly to the scantiness thou hast created—with all thy great works about thee, little hast thou left to give, either to the scithe or to the sickle—but to that little, thou grantest safety and protection; and sweet are the dwellings which stand so shelter'd.

Let the way-worn traveller vent his complaints upon the sudden turns and dangers of your roads—your rocks—your precipices—the difficulties of getting up—the horrors of getting down—mountains impracticable—and cataracts, which roll down great stones from their summits, and block up his road.—The peasants had been all day at work in removing a fragment of this kind between St. Michael and Madane; and by the time my voiturin got to the place, it wanted full two hours of compleating before a passage could any how be gain'd: there was nothing but to wait with patience—'twas a wet and tempestuous night; so that by the delay, and that together, the voiturin found himself obliged to take up five miles short of his stage at a little decent kind of an inn by the road side.

I forthwith took possession of my bed-chamber—got a good fire—order'd supper; and was thanking heaven it was no worse—when a voiture arriv'd with a lady in it and her servant-maid.

As there was no other bed-chamber in the house, the hostess, without much nicety, led them into mine, telling them, as she usher'd them in, that there was no body in it but an English gentleman—that there were two good beds in it, and a closet within the room which held another—

the accent in which she spoke of this third bed did not say much for it—however, she said, there were three beds and but three people—and she durst say, the gentleman would do any thing to accommodate matters.—I left not the lady a moment to make a conjecture about it—so instantly made a declaration I would do any thing in my power.

As this did not amount to an absolute surrender of my bed-chamber, I still felt myself so much the proprietor, as to have a right to do the honours of it—so I desired the lady to sit down—pressed her into the warmest seat—call'd for more wood—desired the hostess to enlarge the plan of the supper, and to favour us with the very best wine.

The lady had scarce warm'd herself five minutes at the fire, before she began to turn her head back, and give a look at the beds; and the oftener she cast her eyes that way, the more they return'd perplex'd—I felt for her—and for myself; for in a few minutes, what by her looks, and the case itself, I found myself as much embarrassed as it was possible the lady could be herself.

That the beds we were to lay in were in one and the same room, was enough simply by itself to have excited all this—but the position of them, for they stood parallel, and so very close to each other as only to allow space for a small wicker chair betwixt them, render'd the affair still more oppressive to us—they were fixed up moreover near the fire, and the projection of the chimney on one side, and a large beam which cross'd the room on the other, form'd a kind of recess for them that was no way favourable to the nicety of our sensations—if any thing could have added to it, it was, that the two beds were both of 'em so very small, as to cut us off from every idea of the lady and the maid lying together which in either of them, could it have been feasible, my lying besides them, tho' a thing not to be wish'd, yet there was nothing in it so terrible which the imagination might not have pass'd over without torment.

As for the little room within, it offer'd little or no consolation to us; 'twas a damp cold closet, with a half dismantled window shutter, and with a window which had neither glass or oil paper in it to keep out the tempest of the night. I did not endeavour to stifle my cough when the lady gave a peep into it; so it reduced the case in course to this alternative—that the lady should sacrifice her health to her feelings, and take up with the closet herself, and abandon the bed next mine to her maid, or that the girl should take the closet, &c. &c.

The lady was a Piedmontese of about thirty, with a glow of health in her cheeks; the maid was a Lyonoise of twenty, and as brisk and lively a French girl as ever moved.—There were difficulties every way—and the obstacle of the stone in the road, which brought us into the distress, great as it appeared whilst the peasants were removing it, was but a pebble to what lay in our ways now—I have only to add, that it did not lessen the weight which hung upon our spirits, that we were both too delicate to communicate what we felt to each other upon the occasion.

We sat down to supper; and had we not had more generous wine to it than a little inn in Savoy could have furnish'd, our tongues had been tied up, till necessity herself had set them at liberty—but the lady having a few bottles of Burgundy in her voiture sent down her fille de chambre for a couple of them; so that by the time supper was over, and we were left alone, we felt ourselves inspired with a strength of mind sufficient to talk, at least, without reserve upon our situation. We turn'd it every way, and debated and considered it in all kinds of lights in the course of a two hours negociation; at the end of which the articles were settled finally betwixt us, and stipulated for in form and manner of a treaty of peace—and, I believe with as much religion and good faith on both sides, as in any treaty which has yet had the honour of being handed down to posterity.

They were as follows:

First. As the right of the bed-chamber is in Monsieur, and he thinking the bed next to the fire to be the warmest, he insists upon the concession on the lady's side of taking up with it.

Granted, on the part of Madame; with a proviso, That as the curtains of that bed are of a flimsy transparent cotton, and appear likewise too scanty to draw close, that the fille de chambre shall fasten up the opening, either by corking pins, or needle and thread, in such manner as shall be deemed a sufficient barrier on the side of Monsieur.

2dly. It is required on the part of Madame, that Monsieur shall lay the whole night through in his robe de chambre.

Rejected: inasmuch Monsieur is not worth a robe de chambre; he having nothing in his portmanteau but six shirts and a black silk pair of breeches.

The mentioning the silk pair of breeches made an entire change of the article—for the breeches were accepted as an equivalent for the robe de chambre; and so it was stipulated and agreed upon that I should lie in my black silk breeches all night.

3dly. It was insisted upon, and stipulated for by the lady, that after Monsieur was got to bed, and the candle and fire extinguished, that Monsieur should not speak one single word the whole night.

Granted; provided Monsieur's saying his prayers might not be deem'd an infraction of the treaty.

There was but one point forgot in this treaty, and that was the manner in which the lady and myself should be obliged to undress and get to bed—there was one way of doing it, and that I leave to the reader to devise; protesting as I do it, that if it is not the most delicate in nature, 'tis the fault of his own imagination—against which this is not my first complaint.

Now, when we were got to bed, whether it was the novelty of the situation, or what it was, I know not, but so it was, I could not shut my eyes; I tried this side and that, and turn'd and turn'd again, till a full hour after midnight, when Nature and patience both wearing out—O my God! said I—

—You have broke the treaty, Monsieur, said the lady, who had no more slept than myself.—I begg'd a thousand pardons, but insisted it was no more than an ejaculation— she maintain'd 'twas an entire infraction of the treaty—I maintain'd it was provided for in the clause of the third article.

The lady would by no means give up her point, tho' she weakened her barrier by it; for in the warmth of the dispute, I could hear two or three corking pins fall out of the curtain to the ground.

Upon my word and honour, Madame, said I— stretching my arm out of bed, by way of asseveration—

—(I was going to have added, that I would not have trespass'd against the remotest idea of decorum for the world)—

—But the fille de chambre hearing there were words between us, and fearing that hostilities would ensue in course, had crept silently out of her closet, and it being totally dark, had stolen so close to our beds, that she had got herself into the narrow passage which separated them, and had advanc'd so far up as to be in a line betwixt her mistress and me—

So that when I stretch'd out my hand, I caught hold of the fille de chambre's . . .

10

Snow on the Lychee Tree

It was 2 January 1945, and I'd been 'home' from school for over a month, living with my mother and stepfather in a rented bungalow on the outskirts of Dehradun. We were surrounded by mango trees and an orchard of lychee and guava trees. Dehra's flora is quite sub-tropical compared to the more temperate vegetation on the hills rising to the north.

Just as twilight descended over the Doon it began to snow. It hadn't snowed in Dehra for over forty years, according to old Miss Kellner who had spent most of her life in the town. This freak snowfall then was something of a sensation, and people ran out of their homes and shops to witness the snowflakes settling on trees, cars and bullock carts. The train from Delhi had to stop several kilometres outside the station because the tracks were buried in snow.

I was in the garden when large, fluffy snowflakes settled on my head and shoulders. It was the first time I was seeing snow. Filled with wonder, I watched it settle on the branches of the lychee trees and on the hollyhocks and sunflowers in the garden. I ran indoors to tell my mother what was happening. She was in bed with my baby half-brother who had come into the world the day before.

'Mum!' I shouted. 'It's snowing outside!'

My mother wasn't impressed, 'I'm not in the mood for your silly jokes,' she said. 'Do something useful. Go and fill my hot water bottle.'

But instead of doing something useful (which never appealed to me), I went outside, broke off a snow-covered branch from a lychee tree, and brought it in to show my mother. She believed me then.

It snowed for a couple of hours, transforming our small valley town into a Dickensian Christmas scene—trees and rooftops all sparkling as the moon came up over the distant mountains. It would never snow in Dehra again.

The next morning the sun came out and the snow melted rapidly. By ten o'clock Dehra was back to normal.

Abnormal snowfalls and freezing winters have inspired many writers, from Chekhov to Dickens and Robert Frost. Virginia Woolf's description of the Great Thames Frost in her historical novel *Orlando* is one that I have never been able to forget. The human race always thinks it can get the better of the natural world; but nature will turn the tables on us when least expected, as we shall see in the following excerpt . . .

From *Orlando* (1929)
by Virginia Woolf

The Great Thames Frost

The Great Frost was, historians tell us, the most severe that has ever visited these islands. Birds froze in mid-air and fell like stones to the ground. At Norwich a young countrywoman started to cross the road in her usual robust health, and was seen by the onlookers to turn visibly to powder and be blown in a puff of dust over the roofs as the icy blast struck her at the street corner. The mortality among sheep and cattle was enormous. Corpses froze and could not be drawn from the sheets. It was no uncommon sight to come upon a whole herd of swine frozen immovable upon the road. The fields were full of shepherds, ploughmen, teams of horses, and little bird-scaring boys all struck stark in the act of the moment, one with his hand to his nose, another with the bottle to his lips, a third with a stone raised to throw at the raven who sat, as if stuffed, upon the hedge within a yard of him. The severity of the frost was so extraordinary that a kind of petrifaction sometimes ensued;

and it was commonly supposed that the great increase of rocks in some parts of Derbyshire was due to no eruption, for there was none, but to the solidification of unfortunate wayfarers who had been turned literally to stone where they stood. The Church could give little help in the matter, and though some land-owners had these relics blessed, the most part preferred to use them either as landmarks, scratching posts for sheep, or, when the form of the stone allowed, drinking-troughs for cattle, which purposes they serve, admirably for the most part, to this day.

But while the country people suffered the extremity of want, and the trade of the country was at a standstill, London enjoyed a carnival of the utmost brilliancy. The Court was at Greenwich, and the new King seized the opportunity that his coronation gave him to curry favour with the citizens. He directed that the river, which was frozen to a depth of twenty feet and more for six or seven miles on either side, should be swept, decorated, and given all the semblance of a park or pleasure ground, with arbours, mazes, alleys, drinking booths, etc., at his expense. For himself and the courtiers, he reserved a certain space immediately opposite the Palace gates; which, railed off from the public only by a silken rope, became at once the centre of the most brilliant society in England. Great statesmen, in their beards and ruffs, dispatched affairs of state under the crimson awning of the Royal Pagoda. Soldiers planned the conquest of the Moor and the downfall of the Turk in striped arbours surmounted by plumes of ostrich feathers. Admirals strode up and down the narrow pathways, glass in hand, sweeping the horizon and telling stories of the north-west passage and the Spanish Armada. Frozen roses fell in showers when the queen and her ladies walked abroad. Coloured balloons hovered motionless in the air. Here and there burnt vast bonfires of cedar and oak wood, lavishly salted, so that the flames were of green, orange, and purple fire. But however fiercely they burnt, the heat was not enough to melt the ice which, though of singular transparency, was yet of the hardness of steel. So clear indeed was it that there could be seen, congealed at a depth of several feet, here a porpoise, there a flounder. Shoals of eels lay motionless in a trance, but whether their state was one of death or merely of suspended animation which the warmth would revive puzzled the philosophers. Near London Bridge, where the river had frozen to a depth of some twenty fathoms, a wrecked wherry boat was plainly visible, lying on the bed of the river where it had sunk last autumn, overlaid with apples. The old bumboat woman, who was carrying her fruit to market on the Surrey side, sat there in her plaids and farthingales with her lap full of apples, for all the world as if she were about to serve a customer, though a certain blueness about the lips hinted the truth. 'Twas a sight King James specially liked to look upon, and he would bring a troupe of courtiers to gaze with him. In short, nothing could exceed the brilliancy and gaiety of the scene by day. But it was at night that the carnival was at its merriest. For the frost continued unbroken; the nights were of perfect stillness; the moon and stars blazed with the hard fixity of diamonds, and to the fine music of flute and trumpet the courtiers danced . . .

It was an evening of astonishing beauty. As the sun sank, all the domes, spires, turrets, and pinnacles of London rose in inky blackness against the furious red sunset clouds. Here was the fretted cross at Charing; there the dome of St. Paul's; there the massy square of the Tower buildings; there, like a grove of trees stripped of all leaves save a knob at the end, were the heads on the pikes at Temple Bar. Now the Abbey windows were lit up, and burnt like a heavenly, many-coloured shield (in Orlando's fancy); now all the west seemed a golden window, with troops of angels (in Orlando's fancy again) passing up and down the heavenly stairs perpetually. All the time they seemed to be skating on fathomless depths of air, so blue the ice had become; and so glassy smooth was it that they sped quicker and quicker to the city with the white gulls circling about them, and cutting in the air with their wings the very same sweeps that they cut on the ice with their skates.

All the colour, save the red of Orlando's cheeks, soon faded. Night came on. As the orange light of sunset vanished, it was succeeded by an astonishing white glare from the torches, bonfires, flaming cressets, and other devices by which the river was lit up, and the strangest transformation took place. Various churches and noblemen's palaces, whose fronts were of white stone, showed in streaks and patches as if floating on the air. Of St. Paul's, in particular, nothing was left but a gilt cross. The Abbey appeared like the grey skeleton of a leaf. Everything suffered emaciation and transformation. As they approached the carnival they heard a deep note like that struck on a tuning-fork, which boomed louder and louder until it became an uproar. Every now and then a great shout followed a rocket into the air: flowering rockets, crescents, serpents, a crown. At one moment the woods and distant hills showed green as on a summer's day; the next all was winter and blackness again.

By this time Orlando and the Russian Princess were close to the Royal enclosure, and found their way barred by a great crowd of the common people, who were pressing as near to the silken rope as they dared. The couple lingered there, shouldered by apprentices, tailors, fishwives, horse dealers, coney catchers, starving scholars, maid-servants in their wimples, orange girls, ostlers, sober citizens, bawdy tapsters, and a crowd of little ragamuffins such as always haunt the outskirts of a crowd, screaming and scrambling among people's feet—all the riff-raff of the London streets indeed was there, jesting and jostling, here casting dice, telling fortunes, shoving, tickling, pinching; here uproarious, there glum; some of them with mouths gaping a yard wide; others as little reverent as daws on a housetop; all as variously rigged out as their purse or stations allowed.

It grew dark. With a burst of passion he snatched Sasha to him and hissed in her ear, "Jour de ma vie!" It was their signal. At midnight they would meet at an inn near Blackfriars. Horses waited there. Everything was in readiness for their flight. So they parted—she to her tent, he to his. It still wanted an hour of the time.

Long before midnight Orlando was in waiting. The night was of so inky a blackness that a man was on you before he could be seen, which was all to the good; but it was also of the most solemn stillness, so that a horse's hoof, or a child's cry, could be heard at a distance of half a mile. The street lanterns in these purlieus were few at most, and the negligence of the night watchman often suffered them to expire long before dawn. The darkness then became even deeper than before. Orlando looked to the wicks of his lantern, saw to the saddle-girths, primed his pistols; examined his holsters. He listened to every footfall; speculated on every sound. Yet he had no fear for Sasha. Her courage made nothing of the adventure. She would come alone, in her cloak and trousers, booted like a man. Light as her footfall was, it would hardly be heard, even in this silence.

So he waited in the darkness. Suddenly he was struck in the face by a blow, soft yet heavy, on the side of his cheek. So struck with expectation was he that he started and put his hand to his sword. The blow was repeated a dozen times on forehead and cheek. The dry frost had lasted so long that it took him a minute to realize that these were raindrops falling; the blows were the blows of the rain. At first they fell slowly, deliberately, one by one. But soon the six drops became sixty; then six hundred; then ran themselves together in a steady spout of water. It was as if the hard and consolidated sky poured itself forth in one profuse fountain. In the space of five minutes Orlando was soaked to the skin.

Hastily putting the horses under cover, he sought shelter beneath the lintel of the door, whence he could still observe the courtyard. The air was thicker now than ever, and such a steaming and droning rose from the downpour that no footfall of man or beast could be heard above it. The roads, pitted as they were with great holes, would be under water, and perhaps impassable. But of what effect this would have upon their flight he scarcely thought. Suddenly, with an awful and ominous noise, a voice full of horror and alarm, which raised every hair of anguish in Orlando's soul, St. Paul's struck the first stroke of midnight. Four times more it struck remorselessly. With the superstition of a lover Orlando had made out that it was on the sixth stroke that she would come. But the sixth stroke echoed away, and the seventh came, and the eighth, and to his apprehensive mind they seemed notes first heralding and then proclaiming death and disaster. When the twelfth struck he knew that his doom was sealed. Other clocks struck, jangling one after another. The whole world seemed to ring with the news of her deceit and his derision. He was bitten by a swarm of snakes, each more poisonous than the last. He stood in the doorway in the tremendous rain without moving. The downpour rushed on. In the thick of it great guns seemed to boom. Huge noises, as of the tearing and rending of oak trees, could be heard. There were also wild cries and terrible inhuman groanings. But Orlando stood there immovable till Paul's clock struck two, and then, crying aloud with an awful irony, and all his teeth showing, "Jour de ma vie!" he dashed the lantern to the ground, mounted his horse, and galloped he knew not where.

Some blind instinct, for he was past reasoning, must have driven him to take the river bank in the direction of the sea, for when the dawn broke, which it did with unusual suddenness, the sky turning a pale yellow and the rain almost ceasing, he found himself on the banks of the Thames off Wapping. Now a sight of the most extraordinary nature met his eyes. Where, for three months and more, there had been solid ice of such thickness that it seemed permanent as stone, and a whole gay city had been stood on its pavement, was now a race of turbulent yellow waters. The river had gained its freedom in the night. It was as if a sulphur spring (to which view many philosophers inclined) had risen from the volcanic regions beneath and burst the ice asunder with such vehemence that it swept the huge and massy fragments furiously apart. The mere look of the water was enough to turn one giddy. All was riot and confusion. The river was strewn with icebergs. Some of these were as broad as a bowling green and as high as a house; others no bigger than a man's hat but most fantastically twisted. Now would come down a whole convoy of ice blocks, sinking everything that stood in their way. Now, eddying and swirling like a tortured serpent, the river would seem to be hurtling itself between the fragments and tossing them from bank to bank, so that they could be heard smashing against the piers and pillars. But what was the most awful and inspiring of terror was the sight of the human creatures who had been trapped in the night and now paced their twisting and precarious islands in the utmost agony of spirit. Whether they jumped into the flood or stayed on the ice their doom was certain. Sometimes quite a cluster of these poor creatures would come down together, some on their knees, others suckling their babies. One old man seemed to be reading aloud from a holy book. At other times, and his fate perhaps was the most dreadful, a solitary wretch would stride his narrow tenement alone. As they swept out to sea some could be heard crying vainly for help, making wild promises to amend their ways, confessing their sins, and vowing altars and wealth if God would hear their prayers. Others were so dazed with terror that they sat immovable and silent, looking steadfastly before them. One crew of young watermen or post-boys, to judge by their liveries, roared and shouted the lewdest tavern songs, as if in bravado, and were dashed against a tree and sunk with blasphemies on their lips. An old nobleman—for such his furred gown and golden chain proclaimed him— went down not far from where Orlando stood, calling vengeance upon the Irish rebels, who, he cried with his last breath, had plotted this devilry. Many perished clasping some silver pot or other treasure to their breasts, and at least a score of poor wretches were drowned by their own cupidity, hurling themselves from the bank into the flood rather than let a gold goblet escape them, or see before their eyes the disappearance of some furred gown. For furniture, valuables, possessions of all sorts were carried away on the icebergs. Among other strange sights was to be seen a cat suckling its young; a table laid sumptuously for a supper of twenty; a couple in bed; together with an extraordinary number of cooking utensils.

Dazed and astounded, Orlando could do nothing for some time but watch the appalling race of waters as it hurled itself past him. At last, seeming to recollect himself, he clapped spurs to his horse and galloped hard along the river bank in the direction of the sea. Rounding a bend of the river, he came opposite that reach where, not two days ago, the ships of the Ambassadors had seemed immovably frozen. Hastily he made count of them all—the French, the Spanish, the Austrian, the Turk. All still floated, though the French had broken loose from her moorings, and the Turkish vessel had taken a great rent in her side and was fast filling with water. But the Russian ship was nowhere to be seen. For one moment Orlando thought it must have foundered; but, raising himself in his stirrups and shading his eyes, which had the sight of a hawk's, he could just make out the shape of a ship on the horizon. The black eagles were flying from the masthead. The ship of the Muscovite Embassy was standing out to sea.

Flinging himself from his horse, he made, in his rage, as if he would breast the flood. Standing knee-deep in water, he hurled at the faithless woman all the insults that have ever been the lot of her sex. Faithless, mutable, fickle, he called her; devil, deceiver; and the swirling waters took his words and tossed at his feet a broken pot and a little straw.